CW00801811

The Pagan's Muse

The Pagan's Muse

Words of Ritual, Invocation, and Inspiration

JANE RAEBURN

CITADEL PRESS
Kensington Publishing Corp.
www.kensingtonbooks.com

CITADEL PRESS BOOKS are published by

Kensington Publishing Corp.
850 Third Avenue
New York, NY 10022

All Kensington titles, imprints, and distributed lines are available at
special quantity discounts for bulk purchases for sales promotions,
premiums, fund-raising, educational, or institutional use. Special book
excerpts or customized printings can also be created to fit specific
needs. For details, write or phone the office of the Kensington special
sales manager: Kensington Publishing Corp., 850 Third Avenue, New
York, NY 10022, attn: Special Sales Department; phone 1-800-221-2647.

CITADEL PRESS and the Citadel logo are Reg. U.S. Pat. & TM Off.

First printing: September 2003

10 9 8 7 6 5 4 3 2 1

Library of Congress Control Number: 2003100139

ISBN 0-8065-2440-5

CONTENTS

꙳ ꙳ ꙳

Acknowledgments

First, I wish to thank all the poets who submitted work for this anthology, who shared their words and their spirit. Their generosity and talent have made this project a joy. I am especially indebted to Cynthia Jane Collins for her excellent perspective and assistance. I also offer sincere thanks to Pat Arant for her gracious hospitality at a crucial time and for writing me poems when I was a child; to Elaine Will Sparber at Citadel Press for her help and advice; to John Belham-Payne of the Centre for Pagan Studies for permission to reprint "Charge of the Goddess"; to Kerry Robinson for her perspective on chants and songs; to Rita Moran and Eric Robbins of Apple Valley Books, as well as to all the booksellers who have been kind enough to support my work; and most of all to Cassius for his wisdom, support, and love, for playing Poohsticks, and for giving me a kitten when I didn't know I needed one.

"THINE INMOST DIVINE SELF"

AN INTRODUCTION
TO PAGAN POETRY

W ho needs poetry? Pagans do.

In most of Western society, poetry is marginal at best. For today's Wiccans and Pagans, poetry is essential. We have many books of ritual, but no standard liturgy. Instead, we have the freedom—and the responsibility— to craft our own rituals. We must choose words that connect us with the Divine, nurture our spirits, and challenge us to become more aware. Good poems do all this and more.

Unlike members of more conventional faiths, Pagans need not—often cannot—follow along in the book, sticking comfortably to another's words. We must choose the words we use to express our spiritual truths, must consider and study those truths, then search for ways to bring them to life. It is work, no more and no less, though it is often work that feeds our souls, hearts, and minds.

This book is a sampling of poetry for (and in many cases by) Pagans. It has two purposes: first, to offer a helpful resource for the ritual writer; second, to inspire readers on their own spiritual journeys.

The poems here were selected both from hundreds

that were submitted for this book and from older works that were suggested to me. The criterion was simple: If a poem seemed to connect to the Pagan spirit, offering a new perspective or thoughtful outlook on our religion, practice, or life, it belonged here. As with any such selection, it cannot help but be subjective and biased. There are many worthwhile poems that are not offered here simply because space did not allow.

The poems here are divided into several sections to assist the ritual writer. The titles of the sections are taken from the "Charge of the Goddess," by the late Doreen Valiente, perhaps the closest thing to a sacred text in Wicca or Paganism.

Some of the poets here may be known to you from festivals and workshops, or from the shelves of your bookstore. Others are seeing their words in print for the first time. Some are longtime, much-honored practitioners of Pagan religions; others are expressing the joys of having just found their spiritual path. Many poets represented here are not Pagan at all; I didn't require any professions of faith, but judged only how well their poems expressed ideas meaningful to Pagans.

If you look to this book for a coherent viewpoint on Pagan theology and practice, you won't find it. Paganism is a path of individuality and intuition, and Pagans' opinions on the proper ways to worship, live, love, and grieve differ widely. I don't agree with every perspective expressed in these poems, but I honor the poets' right to disagree with me, and share their work because I believe it has value.

What Can I Do with Poetry?

A powerful poem can bring light and energy to a ritual, can come close to expressing the inexpressible essence of a magical or divine experience in words. A poem can be a work of magic in itself, seeming to change reality through words.

If you cannot find a poem that suits your religious or spiritual purpose, you may find that reading poetry helps to awaken your senses and empower you to write your own. This in itself can be a ritual or an act of devotion. Experienced Pagans often find that the work of writing poetry—of defining a feeling or thought or spirit, choosing the right words, rewriting and choosing again—makes the difference between a ceremony that goes through the motions and one that changes lives.

Most Pagans, even those who spend much of their time working in groups, practice their spirituality alone, and such a practice can help energize and bring meaning to every part of the practitioner's life. Yet many people get "blocked" when devising rituals, meditations, or magic for themselves. Poetry is a way to unblock the mind, to access those parts of yourself that may not get much energy at your job or in class or while dealing with everyday stresses.

Of course, you can simply read this book for enjoyment or dip into it when you feel drawn to poetry. Here are some ideas for more structured ways you might choose to incorporate poetry into your spiritual life:

 ℛ Choose a poem from this book and bring it with you to a quiet place. Read it over two or three times, perhaps aloud, then spend several minutes in meditation. Notice the ideas and images that the poem evokes.

 ℛ Bring poems to your sacred space and read them aloud as offerings to the goddesses and gods of your worship.

 ℛ Try a "poetry ritual" with your coven or study group, with each participant choosing or writing a poem to represent a part of the rite.

✤ Create a sacred space in your writing area and ask a god or goddess of inspiration to bless your words.

In the end, poetry is for you, the reader, and only you can decide how best to enjoy it. If this book helps bring you closer to your words and your spirit, I can ask for nothing better.

The Pagan's Muse

1.

"I Have Been with Thee from the Beginning"

POEMS OF RITUAL AND DEVOTION

In this chapter are poems that offer homage to a deity or that otherwise lend themselves most closely to use in ritual. Included are poems suitable for creating sacred space and poems intended to sharpen a practitioner's awareness of the deity being summoned.

Charge of the Goddess
Doreen Valiente

Listen to the words of the Great Mother, who was of old also called Artemis; Astarte; Dione; Melusine; Aphrodite; Cerridwen; Dana; Arianrhod; Bride; and by many other names:

Whenever ye have need of anything, once in the month, and better it be when the Moon be full, then shall ye assemble in some secret place and adore the spirit of me, who am Queen of all witcheries.

There shall ye assemble, ye who are fain to learn all sorcery, yet have not won its deepest secrets: to those shall I teach things that are as yet unknown.

And ye shall be free from slavery, and as a sign that ye are really free ye shall be naked in your rites; and ye shall dance, sing, feast, make music and love all in my praise.

For mine is the ecstasy of the spirit, and mine also is joy on earth; for my Law is Love unto all Beings.

Keep pure your highest ideal, strive ever toward it, let naught stop you, nor turn you aside.

For mine is the secret door which opens upon the Land of Youth, and mine is the Cup of the Wine of Life, and the Cauldron of Cerridwen, which is the Holy Grail of Immortality.

I am the Gracious Goddess, who gives the gift of joy unto the heart. Upon earth, I give knowledge of the spirit eternal; and beyond death, I give peace and freedom, and reunion with those who have gone before. Nor do I demand sacrifice, for behold I am the Mother of All Living and my love is poured out upon the earth.

Hear ye the words of the Star Goddess, she in the dust of whose feet are the hosts of heaven; whose body encircleth the universe; I who am the beauty of the green earth, and the white Moon among the stars, and the mystery of the waters, and the heart's desire, call unto thy soul. Arise and come unto me.

For I am that Soul of Nature who gives life to the universe; from me all things proceed, and unto me all things must return; and before my face, beloved of gods and of humans, let thine inmost divine self be enfolded in the rapture of infinite joy.

Let my worship be in the heart that rejoiceth, for behold, all acts of love and pleasure are my rituals. And therefore let there be beauty and strength, power and compassion, honour and humility, mirth and reverence, within you.

And thou who thinkest to seek for me, know that thy seeking and yearning shall avail thee not, unless thou know this mystery, that if that which thou seekest thou findest not within thee, thou shalt never find it without thee.

For behold, I have been with thee from the beginning, and I am that which is attained at the end of desire.

The Charge of the God
Archer

Listen to the words of the Bright God—Apollo, Lugh, Balder, Horus:

I am he who makes the sap to rise and the vine to climb, the fruit to swell and to burst, the blood to rise in woman and in man, and their bodies to put forth milk and honey. I am the sun shining and the rain falling. I am Life. I enter in wherever I please and at my approach all hearts are made glad.

But hear the words of the Dark Lord—Hades, Dis, Arawn, Osiris. And listen to the words of the Dying God—Adonis, Dionysus, Christ. Listen to the words of the Secret God, who spreads his wings within you:

I am the guide to darkness and the father of your initiation. I have gone before you into death and I will lead you through to its end. I have died for you. I have died with you. And now I stand, Lord of the Dead, ready to receive you, ready to let you go.

Come to me when you are ready, and know the mystery: I am nothing more than your own unconquered soul, nothing less than Lord of the Universe, Master of Life and Death.

Elemental Blessings
Kiwi Carlisle

Air: I am everywhere. I fill the fleshy pouches of your lungs, I stir all things from the smallest blade of grass to the tallest tree, I cool you with my breezes and destroy you with my storms. Without me you would die. Am I not holy and worthy of praise?

Picks up incense burner and holds it before priestess, who blesses it. Makes the round of the circle censing the perimeter and bowing to each quarter.

Fire: I live in the guarded embers of campfires and the pilot lights of stoves, I spring from the lightning and the hands of men, I warm you and I destroy you. Without me you would die. Am I not holy and worthy of praise?

Picks up candle and holds it before priestess, who blesses it. Makes the round of the circle bowing to each quarter.

Water: I rise from the moist crevices of the earth, I beat on the shores of her body, I fall from the skies in silver sheets. Without me you would die. Am I not holy and worthy of praise?

Picks up vessel of water and holds it before priestess, who blesses it. Makes the round of the circle asperging it with fingers and bowing to each quarter.

Earth: I am your mother. From me come the fruit and grain and animals which feed you, I am your support, and my pull on your bodies keeps you held firmly to me. Without me you would die. Am I not holy and worthy of praise?

Picks up vessel of salt and holds it before priestess, who blesses it. Makes the round of the circle bowing to each quarter.

Lakshmi

Cassie Premo Steele

Water petals on a lotus hold within them all I need:
the clear sky of leaving, the pink inside of dreams.
I call to you while you are sleeping. Wake, I say,
and go. Clean the floors of your new palace.
Become what you will know. Dig beneath the fig tree,
tearing out each weed. Pursue black dirt
until you are bleeding, your fingers red and dripping
new life onto little seeds. It is the price I ask
of your desire, the deal I make with greed:
You will work until your skin sheds twice,
until you are not who you thought you'd be.
And in this incarnation, I will give you
what your former self did want. Instead
of pleading for another, you will fall
upon your knees, now freed. Holy Lady,
you will cry, Great Sage, All Praise.
For you will know, from work and age,
blood and shedding, that what we gain here
comes from other lifetimes, and often oddly fits.
Still you know that blessing is required.
Still you know that this is all there is.

Samhain Dance

Erynn Rowan Laurie

Now is the eve of winter,
    of Samhain
Bones of the dead will rise
    for Samhain

Ancestors call
    from Tir fo Thuinn
Beating wings
    voice of the swan
Dance from sunset
    into the dawn

And the Gods
will dance
in the mist

Blowing wind
    will call them here
Voice of the dead
    will answer our fears

And sing
as we dance
in the mist

Death to death
    and life to life
Form to form
    on the edge of the night

We call
as we move
through the mist

Womb to tomb
    and birth to birth
Warmth of the flames
    upon the hearth

We are held
in the arms
of the earth

Ancestors come
    they hear our call
Dance their bones
    down echoing halls

They rise
like the tide
of the mist

Prayers to a God and Goddess

Jean Sinclair Symmes

Powerful Lord,
save my great oaks from lightning,
spare them once more.
Let your light pass through them
on its electric way.
See how limbs sway, bow to you,
acknowledging your strength.
Leaves plead in anxious fluttering,
a moving monument to your force.
Do not be so angry that you kill
what was here long before my kind,
who are here a bit, then gone.
I kneel to you.

My lady, let us bargain
honestly. Here's my offer.
I agree to serve you, turn wheels,
murmur with beads in hand,
drive carts around my field,
let my worship rise to you like
a grain-growing miracle.
I will speak your name in the market.
Also I will clip choking vines,
feed faithfully, keep the earth fertile,
face east in the morning. So may I ask
that you support my land, not let
pests sicken nor violence destroy it.
Accept my work and praise. Will that do?
Thank you.

Sky Clad (The Satyrs' Song)

Arthur Slate

We have been separate far too long
this land and I.

I've danced in their shoes
sung with a voice not my own.
Now is the time to take off
this judgment cloth.
Strip away the layers
that block out sun and moon.
Shed the strings that keep
Pinocchio a puppet.

I have danced all the dances
and still gotten nowhere
but the key to wisdom
is experience.
I know myself.
I know this skin must breathe.

These pores naked be.
Dancing free,
these feet need the earth
and I shall dance a dance
to naked and joyful noise.

Beltane

Geraldine Moorkens Byrne

The fires were extinguished at dusk;
doused, dampened, across the
belly of the land.
   The last inspiration of twilight,
   fading with the dying rays of sun
   denying the existence of hope.

The rushlights and candles
standing in brown pots
snuffed out with ruthless decision.
   Breathless and wanton
   She welcomes the dark
   finding perfect acceptance.

A rapidness, daringness, derangement
of wood on skinfulness, sinful the way
they dance against the gathering night.
   Cool breath of death
   against overheated limbs
   brushing against mountain ranges.

Hidden the contours of valley and hill
From the eyes of greed and envy
And on they dance still, heavy with desire.
   Pausing with expectation
   refusing extolments of false praise
   insisting on the truth of cruelty.

Til light streaks and nudity is warmed
By the rising sun, colour restored
In a land overlooked
   The mid-time, the time of forgetting
   The removal of knowledge
   The trampling of self.

Til light streaks and reawakens
In a land unobserved, the tumultuous waters
Unaltered in course by the reappearance of light.
   And the union of dark and lucid
   galvanizes the sleeping soul
   of rush bordered lake and pebbled beach

And the call of the curlew opens up
The soft turf and heather of the marshy
straights, straddling the west
   slight lines of silver traverse
   the sleeping Eriu, the stretchmarks
   of rebirth.

The Fires are relit at dawn, reborn
with tongues of merriment
sending messages across the face of god.
   Rivers of silver this time,
   free-flowing, pushing the days out
   So that evening meets dawn.

Yemaya

Cassie Premo Steele

I hold in my hands your water, cupped
over the breaking waves. It releases
from my finger with the wind.

I hold my palms against the wind
and feel your tiny sand drops sway
from my skin and back again.

I let my body enter your waves, warm
with the sun, and bubble, bounce,
and then sink back into your arms.

A baby, belly down and head up,
I crawl over you and you let me
rock upon your breasts, then you tire.

You make me stand to receive your hand
against my face to remind me
that I am only part of you.

I lie back, let my face go under
slightly, feel you hold me up and
rock me, lift me, drop me, love me.

Your salt is salve for my healing
and I let it sting my wounds,
and begin to suck my terror.

Loving takes a rhythm, you teach me
on the shore of your body, giving
wholly, then going out again.

Waiting for the next round, I look up
and see your shy lips, in the dark
around the moon, kiss in bloom.

Your breast, the water, your face,
the night, I leave you for the land
so I can sleep, and wake, and plan.

As We Are but Travelers Here
(for the Nine Noble Virtues)
John Litzenberg (Greybeard Dances)

As we are but travelers here, beneath this canopy of sky
and rooted to this mount of earth, step gently as your
    path goes by.
Remember that beyond the sight that links us all as kin,
and thankful, lift your voice in praise to gods without,
    divine within.

Tho' we may walk for many miles, the journey is itself
    an end;
so, when you pause to rest, reflect, and when you can,
    assist a friend.

Give caution to stray thought of might and careful tend
    the fire;
for once unloosed, the thoughtless flame knows not
    between the rose and briar.
Your word is but your only wealth, and as the coin, the
    source;
spend wisely, know that your needs are few, and oft a
    want may lead to force.

And walk ye proud, but not in spite, resist the urge to
    shun;
for who among us truly knows when paths are ended,
    or begun?

Seek out the truth, where it is found, and finding it,
    rejoice;
and when the darkness hides that truth, give light with
    steady voice.
Again, give thanks for gifts received, as chance has
    made them yours;
for when the gift reflects the giver, that is its reward.

As we are but travelers here, take heed to tread a gentle
way;
for each step shows a different path where wondrous
journeys lay.

Honor to the Goddess,
Lady of Many Names
Karen Ethelsdattar

"Take, Eat, This is My Body
Which Shall Rise in You
& Be Made Whole"

"Take, Drink, This is My Blood
Which is Poured out for You;
The Emptied Cup Shall be Refilled"

In memory of Edith Hamilton

Goddess of the Harvest
the fruit of Whose joy in the return of Your Daughter
sustains us even as You make bleak the earth
at Her leaving

The earth is rent
& Persephone
the Maiden Whose name may not be spoken
is swallowed by the land of the dead

She will come again
in Whose footfalls spring the flowers & the grain
carrying up with Her
dark memories of whence She came

Demeter
Near in our grief
because yearly we see Your own sorrow
ravage the face of earth
& Your Daughter
Close at the hour of our death
because yearly death claims Her

We know hope because we remember
again & again
Persephone healing Herself
& You with Her, rising

Demeter, Mother
We who have lain on Your knees
& slept in Your arms, give You honor
Anoint us & place us at night
in the red heart of Your fire;
we shall not flinch
& let none in terror
snatch us from that hearth.

Anneal us at unspeakable heat
& give us a slow cooling
that pliant we may return
evergreen with the Spring

We your holy grain
honor You not in slaughter
but as we plow, plant our feet, scatter Your seed
in Your Daughter's returning footsteps
& reap

We the threshing floor
Ground of Your Being
where You stand smiling with sheaves & poppies in
        Your hand
watching the winnowing

In the heat of the morning we wake
our parched throats thirsty for the cup of Eleusis
cooling draught of the reaper
Our limbs longing to sway again in the wind
in Your ancient dances

Out of our dreams, our myths, our nursery tales
those ghettoes in which survive Your memory

we behold the Ear of Corn
we know the song You sung
Song of the Sacred Body
Yours & Our Own
& honor You, Lady of Many Names
Maiden & Immeasurable One.

Snake Dance
Lucille Lang Day

In my stone mask
I dance among rattlers,
their dry sound

of grass and leaves.
Thighs trembling,
I stamp and leap.

Coral snakes encircle
my arms—red, purple
scales glowing.

I hold an asp
in my teeth. A slice
of moon, wedged

in the sky, I dance
each night under
snakeskins, dangling

from black trees.
Naked, I dance
in my igneous mask,

hand-carved;
seed, shell, bone, bead
necklaces click.

A shiver radiates
from my spine.
Neck and back

muscles strain
from the weight
of the mask, the pared

down moon
sinking. I hide serpents,
mirrors, my face.

Henge, Barrow and Midsummer Hill
Tony Grist

Henge, barrow and midsummer hill
Are stations in the sacred landscape.
Here the timeless Goddess enters
The times of her tribes. It was lifetimes back
And what it meant we have almost forgotten,
Almost forgotten.

    We killed a child
With great honour and buried her body
Curled like a snail at the heart of the henge
Where earth spirits might rise through her grave,
Follow the curve of the bent bones
And spiral out among villagers dancing
The sunwheel dance that is danced in spring.
A captive ghost, in my meditation,
She takes my hand, but I cannot lead her
Beyond the ring where the magic fixed her.
She will be four years old forever,
And crowned with flowers.

    But all the rest of us
Have to be laid in tribal earth
To be remade by the winter Goddess

Before we come back to the world again.
She is the sow that eats her farrow,
Old bones cracking within the barrow,
But to those whom she fails to frighten
A giver of gifts.

No corpses lie
On midsummer hill, but of all the stations
This is the saddest. The sun beams down
From a purple sky as midsummer's Queen
Hands over her whitening world to death—
The fields by severance and the woods
By slow decay. With her hair combed out
In its red gold sheaves she is perfect strength
And perfect beauty about to fade
As from this moment summer does
And the child will leave its mother and
The long procession wind down the hill.

Three Sides of Shaman

Ellen Benson

Shaman Shape-shifter you walk alone;
Though the woods you travel are rich in life.
Amazonian Hunter, Healing Mother and Destructive
    Crone;
You choose to adorn the chameleon's cloak
And carry many illuminated masks in your knapsack.

You possess the baneful tongue of the Banshee;
Challenging us to face the venom in our souls;
Your tongue, like lightning strikes the tower that is
    society;
It challenges the Gods to sacrifice themselves.
You are the cycle of Life, Death and Rebirth.
Eye of the storm, Dare us to choose our path.

Great Mother you embrace those willing to swallow;
You Nurture those who killed their ego to obtain
    Enlightenment.
If we dare face our internal oracle;
You will nestle us children to your bosom.
We grow in your fostering warmth.

Dare to defy you, the Three Sides of Sage;
And you will curse the ground we tread upon.
If we choose to disregard the teachings of the Triple
    Goddess;
Stale and empty we become as we sacrifice more than
    our ego.
Go on . . . Stare into the eyes of Medusa.
You will be showered with the gift of her wisdom.

Kithairon

Carey Harrison

Take the leaf;
    The inscription
    Awaits your tinted eyes.

Voice the gods;
    The tones
    Await your silent tongue.

Torch the brush;
    The flames
    Await your bare prance.

Taste the grapes;
    The fruit
    Awaits your piercing bite.

Brace the Earth;
    The soil
    Awaits your calming rest.

Kiss the stars;
 The amber
 Awaits your gentle sex.

Life, my Bacchic friend . . . awaits you.

Yule
Michael E. Bérubé

Sol arose newborn!
we four greeted His small warmth
then returned to ours.

Reverie of the Ice Maiden
SuzAnne C. Cole

(The ice maiden was an Incan sacrificial victim found near the top of
Mount Ampato in Peru. Her frozen remains were displayed in a
refrigerated case at the National Geographic Society headquarters.)

I came perfect to womanhood, expecting to be
chosen. My family rich, my life cherished,
no stooped labor in fields, not even weaving—
no scars to mar my perfection, for even
a single stained tooth would bring dishonor.

I left for my bridal burial singing, plumes
dancing on my bright cap, dress striped
with scarlet, gold, violet, and indigo, while
rich silver pinned close the shawl. My virgin
waist cinched tight by beaded belt as though
encircled by the arms of a lover. Leather slippers—
rope sandals are everyday, not for marrying god.

After two days' climb, first the priests offered
two children, a little bride and groom nestled

against maternal earth, so sweetly curled within
their hollow beds, they seemed to sleep, to dream.
Higher and higher then we struggled in too-thin air,
never before daring god's scorching glance.

One final sleep, then morning prayers, feasting,
and, for me, the ritual cup that dulled all regret,
the man I would not love, the babes not nursed.
Solemnly I faced the rising of the sun, knelt,
awaited the blow to transport me to Ampato's icy
kingdom, there to reign with him forever.

Half a millennium later, ripped from
frozen womb, tumbled headlong down
Ampato's implacable ridge, my mummied
corpse gapes hollow-eyed through glass.
Clubbed to death, I hear you murmur, *sacrificial
victim . . . violent, cruel age . . . poor little thing.*

Save your sympathy for yourselves.
I am married to a god . . . always.

Cernunnos Tattoo

Jeff Mann

Walpurgisnacht, and tonight on the Brocken
the folk gather, dancing about the bonfire,
sipping ale and May wine, passing about
pumpernickel and wursts, falling together
into carnal grass.

              In Blacksburg, Virginia, I strip
to the waist, slide into Shaun's chair.
Against my left shoulder he presses
the stencil, and then the needles begin.

   Now I am standing
on that Dorset hillside, in silence admiring

the Giant of Cerne Abbas. I stay on my side
of the protective fence, though what I want
is to lie naked in the grass, upon the Giant's erect penis,
gripping my own.

And here, at Cluny, the altar
they found below Notre Dame. Cut in the stone,
the name CERNUNNOS. No museum guard
is looking, and I touch the god's bearded face, the stag
antlers, the brow, my hand shaking and tingling.

And there,
in the books, photos of the Gundestrup Cauldron,
the Lord of the Animals, crosslegged amidst
deer, clutching a serpent with ram's horns.

And now here,
in my shoulder's skin. Shaun dips the bee-buzz
needles into tiny pots of black, outlining
the beard, the cheekbones, the antler-spread,

and my own beard
thickens, the dark hair feathers and spreads, soft
as new spruce needles, over my chest, my belly, my groin.
High wind rushes through the antlers of the oak,
the marriage of May Eve, God's face
etched into my animal body,
Cernunnos entering the body of His priest.

Ritual Poem #8
Bonnie Wodin

yes, the Earth
go to Earth
Her quiet strength
flows.

Priestess becomes
interpreter

I stand
a vessel traveling
between
experience
and action.

Redbeard
Laurence Snydal

Done with all doing, sure that sure was not,
Knowing that knowledge gnawed at nothing, most
Gods give up. Odin hung on his hingepost,
Swinging and swearing by himself he wrought
Reckoning. What he left not lightly caught
Nor understood. How could old one-eye boast
Of understanding? Where does this Norse ghost
Get off? At Ragnarok? At Camelot?
Ends are in beginnings. If we forgot
That, then what would be remembered? Almost
Nothing beyond names and what we supposed
They named. Odin, knowing that, knew he brought
Himself to himself. Face to face he fought
Farce and false flattery. Upon the post
He postured until hymn and heart and host
Understood his understanding. He taught
Himself to wait and watch the worm that bends
To tongue its tail. Beginnings are in ends.

Gaia
Rena Yount

Shining and powerful, Mother of Mountains,
your song comes to me like a clarion call.

You are the power that does not stand over
but holds and upholds and embraces us all.

No rules are engraven, no law handed down;
the whisper of wisdom must rise from the bone.
The seed of your sacredness blossoms within us;
all that we meet are your kin and our own.

Unending diversity poured out in joy:
you birth us and set us to face the bright day.
Your loom strung with oneness is woven with freedom.
We choose and discover and weave our own way.

In gladness, in sorrow, my paean I offer,
for small hidden streams and the glory of stars;
For the river of life that holds and sustains me,
spring time and wintertime: all that you are.

Offering 2
Cynthia West

Offer the color red, paint it
on the world with breath risen
from ashes of hate and grief.

Offer words. Write understanding
of earth,
of small foxes
curled up under trees,
of bears
visiting night orchards for apples.

Offer heart, lungs,
legs, breasts,
the varied brocade of years,
the sustenance
of all that's been lived

Air

MoonSongstress

Breathing low as the grass through the meadow
Of my mind, She came. Breath of my breath,
She said, exhaling life dew through me and out
The other side of existence. My centre filled to

Its brim with the salty fresh breezes as it drank
Them in with the hunger of wolves scenting prey.
And I awoke to the life of now to stare into the
Eyes of the storm and feel her pass through me,

Leaving sharp traces of her cool knowledge and
Salt-pan crusting thought, rimming my mind with
Its diamond, crystal, biting edge. Teach me, I
Cried after her. But she was gone and though I

Searched, she was nowhere to be found. But the
Pricking knowledge called me and I scratched
Its surface down and down until I reached the
Core of my soul. There I found her deep in my

Centre, waiting the ages out for time's sweet
Wisdom to dawn in the light of my inner eye.
Yes, I am here, She said. Where did you think
You would find me? So I sat at her feet, looking

Into the grey mist of the morning light, and as
The soft edged dawn was born low in my mind,
Understood with the rising of my sun that She
Was me and I should look within for her shining.

The God of the Waning Year

Elizabeth Barrette

Where is the stag of seven tines?
Where is the woodsman of the pines?

Where is the hunter of the fell?
Where is the wizard of the well?

Where is the green man of the leaves?
Where is the reaper of the sheaves?

Where is the master of the maze?
Where is the sun of autumn days?

Where is the god of corn and grain?
Where is the consort who is slain?

Where is the prince of hoof and horn?
Where is the one who is reborn?

The stag has fallen to the bow
The woodsman lays the great tree low

The hunter goes in search of game
The wizard listens for his name

The green man's lying on the loam
The reaper's gone to harvest home

The master stands where center lies
The sun slips down the autumn skies

The god has fallen in the field
The consort lies upon his shield

The prince is past all reach of men
The one is in the womb again.

Vesta
Leondra Apollonaris

Daughter of blood, daughter of earth
she who stands before the blessed hearth.
Keeper of secrets, choose to share
love and protect those who dare.
Goddess of love, Goddess divine
Lady of eminence whose home is her shrine.
Daughter of water, who touches the fire
Who burns full of passion and desire.
Goddess within, Goddess surround
hold and keep safe, that which is bound.
I am yours, as you are mine
As it will be until the end of time.

Catechist druidicus
Daniel Williams

A rough dream bent over thought
    An ancient oak leans its massive arms
Over sun dappled pools   their cobbled stones exposed

When must one honor a tree?

Always as one honors the breath of the lungs
    And embrace its four-foot girth
As if Dionysus himself were a friend
    Awaiting one's cheek upon his chest
To close one's eyes and find within oneself
    An inner vision of oak

Something in bark and moss
    Sucks the warmth of hands of face
Something dark and stained leaches at taproot level
    Grasping stones   pulls me into itself

My legs broaden and extend
　　My beard a lichen　my eyes
Hollows fit for nesting owls

Old father　must we honor thee?

My body bark enshrined
　　My tendril feet seek underground
Sense a nearby river

Do thy leaves glow with mist?
Does a goddess caress them in falling light?
Do thy leaves beat with the fiery pulse of her
Mourning heart in the death of the year?

My face peers out of your trunk shadowed by
　　Raven's wing　ever watchful one

O holy ancient one　I am blessed
Swathed inside you　carried out of
and delivered of myself　be thou
My defense　O breeder of mists
O Fibrous iron soul

My arms tough and gnarled
　　I bend them up
My thighs twist and curve into
　　Powerful boluses
Meld themselves around stones
　　Of the age of glorious ice

Art thou blessed
In darkness?　In quiet flow?
In starlight?　Art thou blessed
In wind　in thunder?

My heart now pulses with the sun's rhythm
　　Each day　each night　a single beat
Each quiet voice of sunrise　of sunset　its murmur

And art thou not
The gorgeous terrible
Power of fire caught
In lichen   in leaves?
Does not the lightning
Of a thousand years
Cleave each year
of your living?

From my mouth there is no voice
    Only the quiet turn of days
I grow hard and grained and fringed
    I stand alone above the slow
Stone dappled river

O sacred being
Does not a spirit
Fly from thee
Carrying thy scent
Down river?
In the dark night
Are not the stars
Eyes
To coldly watch
Its diaphanous flight?

I have walked to myself
    This yellow morning
Following the circle of my life
    I loosen my grasp from around
This tree's girth   stroll its leafstrewn path

Turn once only to look back upon an
    Emerald god in velvet fustian
A god who tucks my face beneath his leaves

May you live long and be embraced
O father   may thy lovely strength long grace the world
And long may your roots find fertile soil in the earth
Of the human heart

An oak stands deep in its own shade
    I find myself deep within its core
Like an acorn in a shell   and its leaves still
    Follow me on a light wind

When I die a small oak will spring forth
    From the soil of my burial
Through its tiny fuse my spirit
    Will explode green leaves
Into a quiet fragrance of shade

Fragment

Sarah Brown Weitzman

Fragmentary Head of Queen Tiyi
18th Dynasty, ca. 1417–1379 B.C.
—Metropolitan Museum of Art, New York City

Those who cannot comprehend the partial,
needing arms, legs, and torso,
even they can infer the completeness
of beauty only from this fragment
of Queen Tiyi's face carved in yellow jasper
for no other stone or metal then known,
not even gold, could begin to suggest
the warm flush of such flesh.

But only this has been left to us
by the careless haste of robbers perhaps
or the toppling envy of Nefertiti
or most probably smashed by the priests
returned to power after the reign of Tiyi's son
the Pharaoh who worshiped the sun.

Akenaten surely watched the Egyptian noon
strike this saffron likeness and recognized
in that radiance what he believed to be God.

As who among us now gazing upon this
time-shattered fragment would not mistake
such beauty for a sign of the divine?

To Lord Krishna
Nilanshu Agrawal

O Lord of perpetual light
Consume the furious inferno of this muddy pool.
Create eternal rainbows in this devitalized landscape.
Be an honourable guest in this sick heart,
Where nothing but the passions of blood visit.
O patron saint, cleanse this voracious pike
With thy hand divine.
Make me aware of the spiritual occultism
With thine song celestial, O Charioteer.
Thence, my heart overladen with eternal springs
And with green grass and cherry orchards
Will sing a joyous song
At the triumph of Lord Krishna,
Whose radiant chariot burnt in darting glory.
On this very burnished chariot
Gave the elegant flute reciter
The Sermon of Karma Yoga.
O Praise thee O Gopala
For thy eternal message of Karma
Saves countless ignorant humanity
From taking an unholy dip
In the slough of passion and friuts.
Thence free from the fruits of action
Enjoy I eternal bliss in the scheme divine.
Nights of storm and days of mist
Trouble me not.
Rather an ecstatic trancelike vision
Affects me with my Lord's blessings.
Remembering thy early life with your childhood mates,
Thy pining for the butter of the fellow villagers,
Thy fascinating flute recital,

Which entranced the hearts of the Gopis
And thy never perishable imprint
On the heart of Brij-dwellers,
I lose smell of my flesh and music of senses.
Rather, I become conscious of my spiritual well-being.
Therefore, O my fellow-men,
Come, rise, clasp thy hands and sing in His glory.
Thence thou too will be roused out of spiritual stupor
And the truer light of heaven
Will burn in your blighted hearts.
And thou will be saved
From the terrible wheel of birth, rebirth and birth.
So, come, rise, clasp thy hands and sing in His glory
Revealed through his song celestial—The Gita.

Praisesong to Apollo

Elizabeth Barrette

Lyre-gifted Apollo,
Nimble of wit and finger,
Hear us, we beseech thee!

Take aim at our enemies,
Archer of bright Olympus,
And pierce their cold hearts
With the arrows of righteousness.
Look into the eyes of unborn days,
O far-sighted father of prophecy,
And send us hints of things to come.
Set the hand of your healing upon us,
Beneficent one, and bid the plagues pass by.

Sun-glorious Apollo,
Summer's fairest, favored friend,
Goldenmost son of gods,
Receive the sounds of our praise
And be pleased with this offering!

Rhiannon

Charlotte Hussey

"A Celtic earth goddess symbolized by the white mare,
Rhiannon was wrongly accused of killing her child. Her
punishment was to sit for seven years at the gates of her
husband's castle and *tell her story to anyone who might
not already know it; she was also to offer to carry guests
and strangers to the court on her back.*"

—"Pwyll, Prince of Dyfed" from *The Mabinogion*

1

Like a Brueghel painting:
a road climbs a granite bluff
to a castle of bold flags,
heraldic animals. She's
hunkered down in the dust
with scraped-off bits of things
brought there by hooves
clopping the inner courtyard,
the gateway. Its metal grating,
where she leans in torn cloths,
a soiled lace cap, frames
her sunken face. Shrunken
by her heavy leather collar,
she staggers to her feet.
"My story," she begins.

2

In a rock cut chamber,
reddish, slightly gritty
like the hollow in a body
where an organ used to be,
she shows me coiled pots,
hand-built of abraded bits
once packed and sculpted into hills
and the crevices between them
where legs joint the groin,
where flesh folds over the belly—

34

I am part shadow, part
semi-precious brilliance.
Quartz and mica highlights
playing over my shoulders,
fired beads on my halter
ward off the blood-darkened cloths
clinging to my thighs: lands
and sovereignty lost,

rubble: jaws and long-bones
heaped on ashy earth,
with the shards of an overturned pot
that once cooked things to perfection.

Forced to carry others
while telling a story not my own,
I fold against myself: range
into mountain range.
My mane of burning lava
germinates new ground

out of which a delta blooms
protected by a cliff face:

I am the earth you rub
across your cheekbones,
which clings as if to a ball
of lacy roots. A grain, tiny
irritant, falls staining
your lip, slipping around
in saliva before it is gone

in this sandstone chamber,
this hollow hill. Light falls
through a smoke hole, chiseled
like a navel into its ceiling: *Dawn*

light pours
into a coiled,
        big bellied pot,
grain by grain,
story by story.

The Garden of Idunn
Birgitta Jonsdottir

She hides her apples
in a wooden box
sealed with magic.

She feeds them to those
who have chosen
to let their souls grow.
So that their flesh
won't wither away.

Feeds them to
the trembling mouths.
She cuts a little piece
from the apple of youth
places it in the craving mouth
so it may be fresh
as her spring flowers.

She walks her garden silently
with the box
well hidden in her heart.
Waters the apple tree
with her tears of empathy.

Pagan Sabbats in Haiku
Danny DiCrispino

Yule
Sun child born again
In the greatest darkness of
Short winter sleeping

Imbolc
Snowflake shining in
The growing day's star slowly
As she heals herself

*

Ostara
They are equi now
Shifting and springing out of
Floral rolling rest

Beltane
Stirred into manhood
The cauldron conceives his light
Gathering flowers

*

Midsummer
All bonfires burn the
Brightest as solstice seeks for
Flame jumping seasons

Lammas
He enshrines his heat
In her bounty always to
Delve into night's slink

*

Mabon
He prepares to be
Unseen as shadows renew
Themselves leaving sparks

Samhain
The oak burns away
Dropping ashes on the ground
Until sun's rebirth

The Green Man Is Watching Us

Leigh Griffith

The Green Man is watching us.
He's more patient than I
Standing so silent
I almost pass by.

Sudden leaf-rattle laughter
Floats high on the air.
Lets me know that He knows
That I know He's there.

The Green Man is watching us.
He is quicker than eye.
One blink—pop!—He's gone,
I turn and I sigh.

Wind-scuttled wavelets
Float on the pond,
Let me know that He knows
That I know He's gone.

The Green Man is watching us
Our fates are as one,
Entwined as the vines
That climb to the sun.

Don't rush through the forest.
Slow down, still your mind.
Peer into the small spaces,
You might see an eye
    (or an ear, or a lip)

Listen to His music,
His laughter, His sighs.
Feel the woods thrumming
As He passes by.

He's there where the squirrels romp
And lazy bees drone.
The Green Man is watching us,
We're never alone.

Llama Sacrifice

Maureen Tolman Flannery

Zonia cradles the black llama's head in her lap
and sings a pentatonic song of herders,
sings and weeps into the dark, soft fur.
This was her favorite.
She had dressed his long neck in ribbons and weavings.
At Pukllay she adorned his crown with *phallcha* flowers
that bloom only in the time of the festival
in the crags at the height of a dangerous climb.

This one was always first to come
when she brought the herd down from the cliffs.
He used to nudge her playfully
as if he had been a bottle-fed lamb,
follow right at her side until they reached the *ipina*,
lead the others into the enclosure as though
he had appointed himself her helper.

Zonia asked the *curandero* to preside at her sacrifice,
release this llama soul that it rise to the *apus*,
nourish the mountain gods and please them.

When he arrives she stops singing
to honor the *apus* with her silence,
holds tightly to the head in her lap
as the shaman cuts a hole below the llama's right rib
and works his right arm into its side,
severs with his fingernail, deep within the warm chest,
the vein to llama-heartedness,
collects black-llama blood in his hand,

then arches his arm into the air
to scatter it red to the sacred mountain,
requesting the animal's swift return.

Now it is done.
Zonia collects the blood,
pours some on the ground in offering
as she stands to face the mountain she has graced
with the life of her favored animal.
Apu Ausangate, holy mountain
that protects and receives all life,
accept the perfection of this black llama
kept for you here and returned to you now.
I ask that he soon stand upright in my corral.
Make my herd fruitful that it multiply.

They share in the liver and heart
before starting to prepare the meat.
Every bone must be saved and buried together
in the sacred corral—that place
where she danced with her animals last Pukllay
danced with abandon as gaiety began to rise
like mist climbing from the valley
and flute players blew the tune
right into llama ears, alpaca ears
and flowers were strewn like confetti about the enclosure.

Inti descends beneath the cliff-rim of the world
and night climbs up the other side.
She stays at the corral
and searches the Milky Way for a familiar shape,
Yaqana, the black llama of the sky,
dark and fine against his outline of stars.

Solstice
JoAnn Anglin

Like the ancients, we worry in the deepest dark and
wonder if the light will return.

Yet the turning wheel of the moon pulls us
forward into future time, and each night's sky
rotates over us in graceful dance.

The goddesses of plenty arrive and we welcome them
with hope to share in their gifts of light, food, health
and good fortune.

We bathe in the moon's rays of love; the rays
saturate us with the chance of well being, rays as tools
to bring peace to our planet, to spread respect and
caring to all the families of humankind as the families
grow in tune with and reach out to each other.

The promise of this year's evergreen to every culture,
color, gender is that we can accept the darkness as
home as much as the light, and

Create hope again as we leave the old year behind and
Trust in the moons and suns of the year to come.

Waning Moon Invocation
Judith Laura

On the wings of the waning moon,
we see the spiral arms of our galaxy,
and you, Goddess, are there.
On the wings of the waning moon,
we sense the spiral within us,
and you, Goddess, are there.

In the smallest of particles, you shine.
In waves of light, you flow.
In the dying of the darkest hole,
you bear the spark of new life.

Slowly fading crescent,
Honored Crone of change
Ancient One of transition,
open our minds to your wisdom
and our hearts to your love.
On the wings of the waning moon,
be with us here now.

The Provincetown Women Drummers
Dorothy Laurence

The Provincetown Women Drummers
wander along the sandy trail
between old roses and compass grass
to the beach at Herring Cove
lugging bongoes, djembes, Afro-Cuban congas
and frame drums with an eight thousand
year old tradition that goes back to Mesopotamia.

Some of the women have children in hand,
rhythm sticks, bells and tambourines
for them to play. Most carry pizza boxes,
brown bags of subs, or coolers with picnics
for supper on these Friday nights after work.
But there is no sense of weariness in this world
as the drummers assemble in a circle
begin to play, slowly at first,
while other drummers are drifting in.

Led by any one of the women,
rhythms change, ripple through the players,

then through those watching, listening,
like the turning of the tide.
Someone initiates their signature beat,
One, two, three, four
One, two, three, four
One, two
One, two
One, two, three, four

Connecting to the rhythm, bodies rock,
heads fling back, eyes close. Drummers
bring the crowd to a different place
where the beach pulsates with ancient energy
and dancers move barefoot in the silken sand,
arms uplifted to the radiance of sun
setting over the Atlantic.

A Song to Mithras
Rudyard Kipling

Mithras, God of the Morning, our trumpets waken the Wall!
"Rome is above the Nations, but Thou art over all!"
Now as the names are answered, and the guards are
    marched away,
Mithras, also a soldier, give us strength for the day!

Mithras, God of the Noontide, the heather swims in the heat.
Our helmets scorch our foreheads, our sandals burn our feet.
Now in the ungirt hour—now ere we blink and drowse,
Mithras, also a soldier, keep us true to our vows!

Mithras, God of the Sunset, low on the Western main—
Thou descending immortal, immortal to rise again!
Now when the watch is ended, now when the wine is
    drawn,
Mithras, also a soldier, keep us pure till the dawn!

Mithras, God of the Midnight, here where the great bull
    dies,
Look on thy children in darkness. Oh take our sacrifice!
Many roads thou hast fashioned—all of them lead to the
    Light,
Mithras, also a soldier, teach us to die aright!

Blessing
Bridget Kelley-Lossada

May your soul be firm and meaty
like the flesh of olives.

May you stare at the night sky
considering miners of gemstones.

May you steer clear of floodlights.

May you live the life of a fox.

May you not know what art really is
so you can write whatever you want.

May you imagine a fireplace
into existence.

May you breakdance.

May you plant diamond earrings
so they can grow into trees.

Ten Ways to Kill a Witch

Tara Moghadam

Draw the blind on moon.
Concrete nature.
Bottle spirit.
Forbid her to grieve.
Give her shoes that pinch the soul.
Outlaw dancing.
One thousand Hail Marys and not one miracle.
Make her choose again and again between her own body
    and her children's flesh.
Hold her down to one small piece of earth.
              Love her and don't leave her.

2.

"Beauty of the Green Earth"

POEMS OF NATURE

Many Pagans believe nature itself is sacred, not a creation of the gods but divinity in its most tangible, knowable form. In this chapter are poems of observation and experience centered on plants, animals, landscapes, and weather.

Treehood
Archer

Reaching up arms and fingers
Don't we wish we had a green myriad
Whispering in the far-off heights?
How not to long for treehood
When our limbs, our shoulders, our fibered selves,
    close-knit, call out our kinship.
The living tree of the body, rivered with veins, running
    with sap-blood.

Wasn't Apollo broken-hearted when Daphne rushed into
laurel before him
And he, left alone, unanchored, could grasp only a
green-leaved crown?

Oh for roots—we're always saying we have them—
And the leafy reach home to light and wind.
For a mind branching and twigging all ways at once,
alive with flying things,
For silent winters and the painful tingle of sap rising in
the thaw.
For all the knowledge that lies in the flesh and in the
bark,
For the long, slow thoughts of trees.

Night in the Desert

Candace Walworth

I've been caught
red-handed
by the full moon
hiking
with finger on flashlight trigger

from under a rock
staggers a tiny black beetle
with headlights
on bright

The Hound of Ulster

Lawrence Schimel

The neighbor's cat has caught a baby hare.
It's still alive, dangling from her mouth
like a kitten while she plays with it.

As I advance she drops her prey
and disappears into the woods,
intimidated rather than guilt-stricken.
The hare, in shock, quivers
where it dropped, but when I near
bolts. I pursue, to check
that it is not hurt, and cannot help
feeling like Cuchulain as a boy,
set to racing after rabbits until he
was fast enough to catch them, fast
enough to elude the blade.
My chase is not long. The hare
avoids me in quick, zig-zagging
bursts, but with my advantage
of cunning and height, I corner it
against the building's implacable bricks.
And as I lift the small bundle of fur,
hold it, kicking in fear, against my chest,
I know that it is far too easy
to feel the conquering hero.

Alligator Abyss

Paul Brucker

If you must come to the water to drink,
I will welcome you with barely a ripple,
with only my eyes, ears and nostrils above the surface.
I have observed the habits of your kind
and can smell you from two miles away.
I have 3,000 teeth
and I am not a fussy eater.

For 200 million years, I dominated the seas.
Fully grown, I was invincible.

In Egypt, you put my head on the body of a man
and proclaimed me the god Sobek.
You wore my teeth for good luck and health.
In Indonesia, every year, you married me to one of your
    virgins.
People you accused of crime were forced to swim the
    river.
I would eat only the guilty ones, of course.
At Kom Ombo, priests adorned me with jewelry,
fed me cakes and honey by hand,
and mummified me when I died.

You saw us by the thousands dance along the shore,
slapping our heads against the water, snapping our jaws,
calling our women to nudge us, bump us
and pour their sweet green oil all over us.

We are as we were made and we can't be made anew.

I nudged my head out of a porcelain-white egg.
Mother carried me to safety in her jaws
which can crush a lion's skull into a thousand pieces.
Raccoons, baboons, birds and bears—even my elders
tried to make a meal of me.
Now it's my turn to eat them.

I can stay under water for an hour
and can last a year without eating.
But that matters little now.

Now that you use my skin as a status symbol.
Now that you carry a mysterious iron
that magnifies me eight times and shoots.

Today, hundreds of thousands of us are raised on your
    "farms"—
a commodity to slaughter, skin and shellac.

Look for my head in the flea markets of New Orleans,
going for $20 a pop.
Look for me, posing in the airport gift shop,
stuffed, with glass eyes—
an English squire in a tweed coat, cane and cap.

My land you continue to drain and bulldoze
for your luxury condos, gas stations and malls.
What's more, you point and laugh at me,
safe behind the glass of your zoos.
And you eat me in chic cafés,
as a meatball or a stew.
My pink-white meat tastes like veal or tuna, you say.

I have watched the woolly mammoth, the saber-toothed
    tiger
and the buffalo come and go.
I do not want to go there.

But when I look to the east, a new day does not come
    to warm me.
When I look to the west, darkness extinguishes my eyes.

So I warn you.
This is my land, my food, my women.
Stay back
or I'll blow bubbles, bellow and lunge.
Sometimes I'll kill you instantly,
throw back my head and swallow you whole.
Other times, I'l take you down and drown you,
then tear you up into bite-sized portions.
Between swallows, I may come up for a little air.

Grace

Karen Donnally

Weakened by overwhelming circumstances,
I barely face living.
Carrying more bills and expenses than I can manage . . .
every link to a punitive, uncaring patriarch
binding me to a sense of worthlessness
so deep I want to die.

A gentle nuzzle of her massive head
nudging its way underneath me
carefully lifting me
off the submerged ground
of low self-worth . . .
whinnying,
reddish-brown coat shimmering
in the glowing strokes of daybreak
emerging over the horizon.

A new thought arising
out of the elevated status
of barebacked equestrian power.
By osmosis, I draw strength
from her four-legged struts
planted deep within the earth
supporting her luxurious, softly-carpeted back
and me.

My arms tenderly wrap around her neck
as it pillows my worries away.

Neither distinction of horse or human
nor judgment or apparent sense of separateness
could endure the perfection
of a moment in grace.

In Broad Daylight
Candace Walworth

Night hides in the bark
of pines under rocks and
between toes

Like a stray cat begging
for milk or bite of fish

night lingers
all day

the dandelion woman
Jessica Jordan Nudel

And she said
I am like the dandelion
wild and free
I travel with the wind
I am seeds and sparrows
I am pulled out by the roots
and I grow again

I grow in fields
I grow on mountains
I grow on bricks
and up through cement
where there is no life
I bring life
where there is
the slightest possibility
I grow

no one plants me
no one plans me
I go where the wind takes me
I carry your wish
in my heart
I scatter myself across
the earth

I grow beautiful with age
I grow white
I grow round and light
I learn to fly

and she said
I am like the dandelion
I am always fertile
I am full of seeds
I am full of
other dandelions

I am full of color
I am full of yellow
I am full of wishes
I am full of dreams

The Storm

Joyce Derzaph

Dark clouds massing
thunder bellowing in the distance
rain, gently beginning to fall.

Building, growing
Moving closer, coming harder
winds begin to blow.

Surging, flashing
feel the energy of the storm
mounting in the bloated clouds.

Crashing, booming
breaking at last over the waiting earth
water pounding the ground.

Slowing, passing over
losing strength as the distance grows
blue skies and sunshine returning

Crisp and clear
nature's power refreshes the air
the dust of the masses washed away.

Predators

Loren Davidson

Grizzly bit me,
Infected my spirit
Hot, predator pulses
Course through my blood
Collect in my heart
Shift my mind's eye
Show me the Web of Life,
The eons-long dance
Of eater and eaten.
Forests rise
And forests fall
And rise again, unending cycle.
Knowing this, I return to my garden
As predator, shaper, steward
Climax of my self-created food chain
Living my borrowed life
Until the day
When my plants eat me in turn.

The Stars Are Also Sisters
Ann K. Schwader

The names of constellations echo women
passed into legend by that twisted path
each exile learns: the quick, too-honest breath
of lust or rage, raw sorrow unforgiven,
a mother's pride which prodded at some god's
own fragile self-importance. Queen or virgin,
heartbroken sister, she-bear still determined
to love her ill-got cub—it's all a plot
& always was. Will be. Survivors scarred
by inconvenient courage, bone-deep weary
we struggle on somehow until the night
delivers us. Past haze of city lights,
we gaze in sacred silence at the body
of Nut Great Mother, thick with sister stars.

The World Is Too Much with Us
William Wordsworth

The world is too much with us; late and soon,
Getting and spending, we lay waste our powers;
Little we see in Nature that is ours;
We have given our hearts away, a sordid boon!
This Sea that bares her bosom to the moon,
The winds that will be howling at all hours,
And are up-gathered now like sleeping flowers,
For this, for everything, we are out of tune;
It moves us not. —Great God! I'd rather be
A Pagan suckled in a creed outworn;
So might I, standing on this pleasant lea,
Have glimpses that would make me less forlorn;
Have sight of Proteus rising from the sea;
Or hear old Triton blow his wreathed horn.

Tree Song
Natalie Green

Earth rooted, twisting, warm in Earth.
Growing straight and tall and twisting,
Bark patterned, ridged and marked,
Knotted, faced, spirits of standing people.

Host of all-heal, lovely, little apple spirits,
Pretty little ones, pink blossomed.
Tiny new leaf filling the Spring.
Green ones, cascading waterfalls of green.

Old, yet young, re-birthed each wheel turn.
Limey green of beech, dark of yew,
Feathery loveliness of ash,
Grace of bending willow, water's friend.

Forests of fir, tall, straight, high ones,
Givers of dark cool places, safe, fragrant,
Bracken floored, cone carpeted, paths
To grove of oaks, native, noble ones.

Warm and wooden, moss barked.
Golden light of life and leaf turn,
Gold, red and falling, falling
Back to Earth, to feed, to grow . . .

I Am the Ocean
Melisande Luna and Michael Bartlett

I am the ocean;
a vastness that writhes
under the eye of the moon.

My frenzied water snatches towns
in tsunami blooms of sorrow,

Diurnal tides swash from me,
churned from prevailing winds of mind,

their crescendo climbs until each wave of me
meets a place to rest,
                              breaks,

and in sighing retreat
I whisper seductive promises
of green rooms, inky depths.

first fruits

mbtucker

the first fruits of the Mother,
   harvest of a ground-running vine,
      born so close to the Earth,
         absorbing Mother's nurturance,
            and returning her bounty to you
               richly red and succulent . . .
                  prepare to know her:

she wears a green cap to mask her shyness;
   she steals glances at you, drawing you into her
                              seduction;
      she wears her seeds as an adornment,
         a dress to cover the red of her passion . . .
            remove her dress with your mouth.

take the milk of her juice into yourself,
   feel her gift of flavor with the tips of your fingers,
      see her sweet fragrance with new eyes,
         smell her luscious curves with a fresh new sense,
            hear her skin give way to your bite,
               taste the release of her ripe blessings
                  to the excitement that is
                     your awakened being . . .

this nugget of life is more than food, more than
first-fruit . . .
as you merge all of your senses with her voluptuous
body,
as you accept her love, her life into yourself,
imagine what else she offers you
in this sacrament of Mother's gift . . .

Blackberries
Susan Kennedy

filled with the sweet, thick
black-red blood of the dying sun-god,
dark taste of lengthening nights
in the full heat of summer.

bittersweet bite and barb
of our own mortality

those who do not ripen fully
remain too red, too hard, too sour,
on the vine, never entering
the sharp-gated, pink-tongued mouth,
to be squeezed and shredded by desire,
to enter the hot blood of the devouring creature
whose opening and closing black center
is ever-scanning for the next mouthful of perfect
purply plumpness, stores for the coming
long cold slumber.

3.

"Thou Who Thinkest to Seek for Me"

POEMS OF INVOCATION

This chapter centers on the point of contact between humans and deities, incorporating both calls for divine presence and poems that may represent the answers to such a call. This chapter is also about the experience of invoking a goddess or god, for that alone can change the one who does it.

Oath of Scribes
Dennis Saleh

after the Egyptian, *The Book of Thoth*

Harken ye I am the Tongue of Thoth
as Thoth is the Tongue of Ra which
uttereth all things before time began
Inscribed with this palette I make words
to Thee Lord Thoth only for thy blessing

Words are my master There is no other
No Man Not any I will believe nothing
before it is written until it is written
or not written well I will believe in
no thing not written I did not write

I will efface no written thing nor cause
to be unwritten anything through
error or substitution Also neither will I
affix my name to the work of another
nor cause nor allow another's to be undone

Also will I observe Shorten not names
of others nor lengthen that of thy own
Do not write other than facing light
Use no thing twice Also will I observe
the forms of *Maat* Measure Balance

Who can write addresses the gods
by name in their own language
words beautiful of Thoth whose
visage is form whose throne is
noon brilliant yellow electrum

And upon that day and in that hour
will I write yet Will I sit at the feet
of death and write what it
death doth say though it be upon
my heart death doth inscribe

There is no thing for that hour
save the breath of words Only
with words cometh man into
the eternal Not ten thousand
eternities make a truer thing

Triple Goddess

Barbara Ardinger

I: The Virgin

The women gather in the light of the new moon.
Listen to their voices:

Holy is the Virgin
Sacred is the Maiden
Her innocence
Her strength
Her independence.

Ageless One-in-Herself, She explores,
She opens and touches
She is the daughter-of-all.

Let us celebrate our virginity, our holy maidenhood
Celebrate our first encounter,
Our wondrous beginnings
Our new growth into all new worlds.
Untamable is our virginity
Untouched is our center.

We are the blessed Maiden,
Full of grace, full of lovingkindness,
Our full potential filling the whole world.
We are beginning, we are opening,
We take our first steps, We are journeying.
We are fierce and fragile,
We are untouched.
We touch all things.

Praise be to the Maiden.
Blessed is She in us.

II: The Mother

The women gather in the light of the full moon.
Listen to their voices:

Praise be to Our Mother
Blessed is her power:
Her blood
Her hands
Her milk
Her womb.

With her, we celebrate our motherhood
Our daughters
Our sons
Our motherlove
Our motherwork.

Mother-of-all, we celebrate you
We celebrate our own mothering—
Our fullness
Our choice.
We celebrate our nourishing nature
Building friendships
Planting gardens
Tuning engines
Touching, persisting, feeding, cheering.

We are the Mothers.
Let us celebrate ourselves:
let us grow, let us bloom, let us reach and grasp and hold.
We are the Mothers:
we have the blood, the hands, the milk, the womb.
We are the builders, the creative ones, the fierce
protective ones.
We have the power.

Praise be to the Mother.
Blessed is She in us.

III: The Crone

The women gather in the shadow of the waning moon.
Listen to their voices:

Praise be to the Crone,
Precious is the Wise and Terrible Mother
She touches all
She destroys all
She nurtures all.

Ageless in Her majesty, she is Grandmother-of-All,
Old woman
Chaperone
Bag Lady
Fury.

Let us celebrate ourselves.
We speak our minds, for we know who we are,
We did that before you were even born,
We've already been there.
We remember.
We are the healers
The judges
The counselors
The ritual-makers
The priestesses.

We are the old ones, bloodless and bloody.
We are the mothers of mothers.
Let us celebrate the Crone in ourselves,
Let us hone our wisdom, test our hunger
Bless our overflowing lives.
We are the untouched, the powerless powers.

And through us
the wheel turns again, and the spiral spins

Through us
Life and death come face to face
And life goes on and on.

Praise be to the Crone.
Blessed is She in us.

Invocation to Artemis
Archer

Artemis
I come to you naked in my armor
Take me into your company
Though you love to hunt alone

I'll hang back
Not upset the dogs
Nor put them off their scent

Find me
In the grove
Crack open this carapace
Find my woman's body
It will be my pledge to you
That I am real
Though I wear this cage on my back
That only you can open

St. Bridget

Sandy Crimmins

To pray at the well of St. Bridget:

Make obeisance on your knees.

Walk three times around the crucifix that stands in the
    courtyard.

Bow twice and say a decade of the rosary at each of the
north, south, east and west corners of the enclosure,
after which you may enter the site on your knees
with your offering in your left hand.

At the well, bow your head, recite the Credo
and ask for the saint's intercession.

Leave your offering
and consider making a financial donation
for the upkeep of the shrine.

Or you could drive up
Park.
And enter the well house.
Simply walk past plaster saints
Decaying in the dank
Ignore the ink-blotched
Tearstained
Damp-run
Prayer petitions
That have been stuck in every corner,
On every statue and picture frame
Weighted to every rock on the floor
Tied to every beam and nail
Walk by all of them
Focus on the early times
Those days when Brigid's reincarnation

Spent her days
Combing moss and whitewashing walls
You can walk right past the please and thank you
Of the black-dressed Saint Bridget
To the omphalos
The womb of Brigid
To dip your hands in her healing well
To say hello, are you there?
To wonder:
As long as we come
Does it matter what sends us?

Hymn to Athena

Raven Kaldera

You were so seductive, Athena,
seductive as you can only be to
an adolescent
others may have embraced Aphrodite or
Dionysus or Hera but I
the child whose home
erupted in daily violence
found your armor so bright and safe
your promises so grand . . .

I outgrew you, though,
when I left home and more earthly
pleasures called,
bowed out of the ranks of glory
went AWOL from the epic—
I, a hero? Never,
the best I'd ever do would be
security and a love-warmed bed
and be grateful.

But now you call me again,
because the world is racked and rent and
it needs saving

even if there are no more heroes,
only weak fools like me who
break too easily under your demands.

And yet, perhaps, lady in armor,
father's daughter, favored son,
in spite of my protestations to the contrary
there are still some lessons
you have yet to teach . . .

Samhain

Louis Elvira

Deep rumbling,
the whine of electric air
the veil opens.

Will you see yourself?
How deep is your faith?
Will the smell of jasmine
find safe haven
in your soul?

Sacred ancestors
who came before
what were your dreams?
Are the summer lands
rich in color and life?
Or are they but half forgotten shades
and dreams?
Will our touch be free
or chained
upon a silver wall?

Tears of gold flow freely
only to turn to dust.
Upon this night we
revel with children gone.

In the morrow
a new year shall ring.

Will it bring a better year?
Or shall we face the obsidian mirror
once more?

Papyrus Wine
Dennis Saleh

1.

Paper is very godly for it is white
and full of promise Paper
was next to godliness in the
first days of the age of pages
when there was greater
understanding of its whiteness
What better for writing down
directions to the desert or to gods
Where better news of paper
than in the past The very first
words were the gods' thoughts
given man to know the glory
of worship and the breath of
providence is upon each page

2.

The papyrus is the Lord God's mirror
and the words upon it are in His image
The song of paper the scribes chant
unrolling sheets and cat whisker quills
in Byblos and Tyre and Sidon is His
praise thanksgiving for the miracle
of the paper the lamp of the sun
and the favor of He who makes all
things as a scroll before the ink

Osiris be Osiris Come and sit beside us
Rhyme with papyrus make it sing
Fill thou page of white this day

3.

And in the shadow of the Nile
the reeds joyous with ten thousand
thoughts of fruition in the seed
And in the night the milksap
fermented by the priests blinded
from vapors in the hidden rite
pours whiter than at noon
than a hundred palace columns
than the moon upon the sands
In the false hour O White
strengthen and reprove us
In the peace of paper is the dawn

4.

Drink the papyrus wine
Take the draught and taste
and the fullness of emptiness
and the presence of nothing
shall be as yours and the ache of gods
And there shall be as no roof
to any chamber and no sky to any day
and no stars to any night
And there shall be as no ceiling
to any temple and no end to prayer
and no end to the ten thousand
words of white which are the names
of the Lord Osiris who blesses
and has mercy upon us

Black Kali

Deborah Hunter

I.

You emerge from the Yoni of wisdom and insight.
Borne from Durga's forehead in righteous indignation,
brandishing sword and noose, head-bone adorned,
you crunch chariots and riders in your teeth;
shatter demon bones with each step.
The earth trembles. Your laughter shakes the skies.

II.

Black Kali who faces South, clad in night raiment
of stars and planets, is free from illusion.
Mouth wide open in glory, tongue at rest,
Dark Mother, creator of the nothingness,
draws all things into the black emptiness that
swallows the light and transforms matter
into perpetual energy.

III.

You sever the bonds of ego,
infuse us with your spirit.
We are baffled by your
raw energy, calling it
savage and indiscriminate,
denouncing it as a blind force that
dances across the prostrate body
of nature, with its tongue
hanging out, slashing
heads and hands like a scimitar,
and glorying in destruction.
An eye guards the door to the past.
An eye focuses on The Now.
An eye navigates the future.
Your tongue on chin, a
red, velvet settee,
teaches me silence.
"Temperance," you warn.

Your own four hands
are not still. They
hold the corners;
create the elements.
Each finger knows its duty
and performs it with calculated ease.
The universe is you
and you are the universe
with fifty hands at your waist,
resonating the cosmos;
hands at work: Karma.

IV.

So it is. So it shall be.
It is complete.

The Dagda
Ellen Cooney

You are the Good God
the lord of the lusty belly full
with Your huge bronze cauldron rich in
mutton potatoes peas and porridge
You are potbellied for the work
full of the waters of life
You are the king and father of all
who wanders the land in piebald rage
feeding the people
with one end of Your holly club
You kill nine enemies
at once and with the other
You restore them to life
over and over
With Your harp You turn
the seasons from the time of
flowers of silver to the time of
leaves of gold

The Fates

Helen Ruggieri

CLOTHIA: THREADS THE NEEDLE

wearing her blue wrapper,
embroidered with a gold dragon
looking on a field of poppies

peels potatoes,
quarters them in
a cast iron pot.

Crow taps at her window
a long red thread in his beak
trailing like a spittle of blood.

She winds it on a wooden spool
waves him away
with a few seeds of corn.

Dinner simmers.
The pond covered by
a thin cataract of ice

except for one spot
by the inlet catches sun,
opens wide as a golden eye.

LACHESIS: MAKES THE STITCHES

steps to the light,
drifts from where she
was sired by Dark

embroiders a serpent
in red on a purple gown,
eyes of fire opal,

tongue ending in a peony,
about to speak,
stirs the stew.

She pulls knots and crossings
an image encompassing
the pewter secrets of her needles.

The nacreous sky opens an eye
of turquoise against
her long thin fingers.

ATROPOS: CUTS THE THREAD

How beautiful the serpent's tongue
she thinks and judging done-ness
dishes out the stew.

Late into the evening
she reads their poetries
wrapped in a black robe,

cobwebs traced in silver on the sleeves,
the collar ringed with lilies
stemmed with a fringe of many threads.

She traces each stanza with her finger,
takes scissors from the basket,
makes the cut.

When embroidery is done,
it's done.
No one argues with her logic.

Above, dark wings of kohl
steadfast against titanium;
there is no wavering.

Helios' Eyes
Ellen Lindquist

Come and embrace
the fields with sun,
Hang down with rain
arms of wind,
Scatter fragments
of water as if
memories are clear
to us now.
Come to be,
be my one,
embrace me now
your eyes the sun.

Oblation
Dennis Saleh

Osorkon VII, Pharaoh, XXIInd Dynasty
To Lady Bast, cat goddess
Temple of Bast, c. 700 B.C.E.

I make thee thanks
    I give thee thanks
For the parts of
    thy body be unto holy
Thy muzzle like unto
    the Delta of Egypt
Thy whiskers like unto
    the papyrus tassel
Thy eye like unto
    minishing veils
Thy ear like unto
    listening of a sea shell

Thy ear like unto
    hearing of a temple bell
Thy forepaw like unto
    the delicacy of a flower
Thy forepaw like unto
    the sanctity of a virgin
Thy back like unto
    the river's flow
Thy stomach like unto
    the deep well
Thy hindpaw like unto
    the rearing stallion
Thy hindpaw like unto
    the lion's haunch
Thy tail like unto
    the shadow of a date palm
Thy fur like unto
    the gentlest balm
Thy purr like unto
    the contentment of Maat
I make thee thanks
    I give thee thanks
Thou thrilleth night
    when thou goeth into it
Thou maketh alliance
    with the moon
Thou filleth the
    darkness with care
Thou inspireth the
    shadowy place
Thou goeth before
    in the hall alone
Thou goeth against the
    enemies of Pharaoh
Thou putteth thy fear
    in the granary
Thou maketh the serpent
    to be expired

Thou maketh the rat
  to be no more
Thou maketh the stores
  to be fortified
Thy claws like unto
  the harvest sickle
Thy bite like unto
  the gate of pain
Thy kicking like
  unto violence
I make thee thanks
  I give thee thanks
Thou seeketh after the
  member of Osiris
Thou giveth Oxyrhynchus fish
  to take care
Thou giveth Mormyrus fish
  to take care
Thou maketh thy home
  in the heart
Thou maketh the
  spirit of Pharaoh glad
I make thee thanks
  I give thee thanks
The missing place is thine
  Thy forgotten place
The lost place is thine
  Thy unseen place
The secret place is thine
  Thy hidden place
The unknown place is thine
  The holy place

Frau Holda

Ellen Cooney

You ride across the blood moon
ride across the white lands
the night between the years
black wolves howling
drawing Your sleigh
Your silver dress shimmering
Your long golden hair streaming
You toss children to barren wives
blue flax flowers to
indigent farmers plump pears
to orchards red stags to forests
jeweled grain to white fields
You sweep away sickness
and bring youthful vigor
You are the Yule tree that
gives birth to all
Yours is the voice
singing in the well

Prayer to Arachne

Bethanie Frank

Weave for me your endless web
We wail over Athena's decision.
Spin a web to set up free
May you show us the way of the spider.
Silently waiting.
Your webs are treacherously beautiful
Your talents remarkable.
Spin forever—we will wait.

He Sets Up His Feet

Ava M. Hu

after "Maximus" by D. H. Lawrence

Outside, the wind crashes around corners.
Outside, women in their black coats sing.
Outside, a small dog crosses the street
and decides to turn back again.

What darkness is there in a stranger leaning on the
        garden gate?
Would you ask him to come in?
Would you call to him, and uncork the wine,
pour out your sugar buckets over bread?
Over there, through that open window,
they say a man lives with glass bones.
He does not need to come outside. He paints

weathervanes, maps of madagascar, the red
cowrie shells of young girls with mahogany-colored eyes.
Would you be afraid if the stranger came in, laid down
        his cloak,
told you his real name? Would you let loveliness
enter you, smile to yourself, saying: He is a god!

God is older than the car parts and wrenches of
this small seaside town. The salt inside
the eye cannot behold him
nor the accordion's voice describe him:
and still, this God Hermes, sets up his winged feet
on your hearth.

Prayer for the Healing of the Mind
Laura Loomis

The Saami people of Scandinavia believed depression and mental illness were caused by the absence of Beiwe, goddess of the sun.

Let the season of ice
end at last.
Come quickly the solstice,
the rising of golden Beiwe
her sunshine melting darkness
like the snow that will slide away forgotten
into water to nourish our souls.

Bird Woman
Cynthia West

Bird woman, humans scare you so,
poised for flight, feet barely touching
an unfamiliar earth, your feathers shake.

Bird woman, eyes slit to see beyond
a world that is not yours, listen wide across
blueness for a call you know.

Bird woman, leap fast from the
fetters of your clay body, outfly
the mistake that you are anything but spirit

Bird woman with face painted for ceremony
and senses stretched sunward, now is
the moment, spread your eagle wings and soar

Bird woman, huge as lightning, dance
with speeding clouds and stars, drum with thunder,
with singing wingbeats join your own.

Hymn to Dionysos

Eric Robbins

Tell us, oh Muse, of one who stands behind me now,
A weaving, stately image there, reflected in
The wine. For "thunderstruck," the poet says, is how
The dithyramb is danced, is how we honor Him.

O Dionysos peel away my outer layers
Of rationality, of intellect that shuts
The inner wisdom off. I raise my cup to You,
And try some steps, and try some words, then dip once
      more.
I'm singing neither cleverly nor clearly, Lord,
But that's your gift; the wisdom of the song and of
The stage is never found upon the printed page.
The mixing-bowl, still nearly full, already shows
Reflected bearded arch-browed inner consciousness.

Say that three times quickly! No two celebrants
Will hear your words the same, but nonetheless you
      speak,
And we will hear, and know your gifts, and sacrifice
A splash of wine, some honey-bread, an hour or three.
With you we live outside our minds, outside of time,
And though your gifts will fade in memory before
Our sacrifice is done, still we return, we dance
The timeless cadences of beasts beside your spring.

Erce: Earth Goddess

Edited and translated by K.A. Laity

These verses come from an Anglo-Saxon manuscript (MS Cotton
Caligula A vii) dating from the late tenth-century England. They form
part of an elaborate charm to return fruitfulness to a barren land. It
would have been invoked at the first spring plowing. The name

"Erce" does not occur anywhere else in the body of Anglo-Saxon poetry, so we know nothing more of this goddess apart from her apparent connection to the Earth. A number of charms with similarly pagan attributes appear in other medieval manuscripts, even though most of the texts were recorded by monks. Unlike many modern Christians, these monks did not seem to feel a need to deny their pagan past. Sometimes pieces of the rituals are Christianized; for example, this charm instructs the farmer to repeat the Pater Noster nine times before facing the east and chanting the pagan verses.

Erce, Erce, Erce,
    Earthen Mother.
May the all-powerful, eternal ruler
    grant thee
acres fruitful
    and flourishing,
increasing
    and strengthening,
in high condition,
    in bright abundance,
and the broad
    barleycrops,
and the white
    corncrops,
and all
    earthly abundance.
Grant to him,
eternal ruler
(and his holy ones
    who in heaven are),
that his ploughing be protected
    against any and all enemies
and it be guarded
    against each and every evil,
against those spells
    sown through the land.
Now I bid the ruler
    who shaped this world,
that neither the conjuring woman
nor the cunning man should

make any changes
to the words thus spoken.

Hale be you, earth,
   mortals' mother!
May you ever be growing
   in the god's grasp,
filled with food,
   useful for folk

Consorting with Ereshkigal
Jennifer Bradpiece

Inanna, Heaven's Queen,
hangs from a meat hook.
She dangles in her sister's realm;
dripping flesh from bone
in willing surrender—
to be stripped away,
to be reborn.

At the fire, the women dance,
together they sing.
They remember their dark sister,
revel in Her wild process.
They reacquaint themselves with
what they knew.
They enter
to be stripped away,
to be reborn.

At her desk, a woman cries and
stares out the window.
Her doctor suggests Prozac.
Her sister prescribes a day at the spa.
Her boyfriend diagnoses "hysteria."
All of them whisper,
quick to name her.

She is consorting with Ereshkigal.
She is a goddess
hanging on a meat hook.

Four Invocations

Tish Eastman

i.

Goddesses of the earth and sky
Spirits of the woods and seas
Gaea, Hera, Pomona, Ran
Let your white light protect me
Let your blue light heal me
From the ills of the unnatural world.
May it harm none.

ii.

Goddesses of the earth and sky
Spirits of the rocks and hills
Isis, Nerthus, Cybele, Nuit
Let your blessings sustain me
Let your strength shield me
From the evils of the unnatural world.
May it harm none.

iii.

Goddesses of the earth and sky
Spirits of the wind and rain
Diana, Selene, Iris, Sati
Let your wisdom wash over me
Let your mercies cleanse me
Of the sins of the unnatural world.
May it harm none.

iv.

Goddesses of the earth and sky
Spirits of darkness and light
Spirits of magic and love
Venus, Hecate, Persephone, Aphrodite
Let your powers purify me
Let your passions awaken me
I ask in gratitude for gifts given.
      May it harm none.

An Invocation to Brigid
(September 11, 2001)

Barbara Arnold

Goddess of fire, protect those who fight.
Goddess of medicine, sustain the healers.
Goddess of agriculture, feed all who toil.
Goddess of mothers, comfort those who lost children.
Goddess of the hearth, heal the burns.

  Goddess of smithcraft, strengthen our mettle.
  Goddess of martial arts, focus our might.
  Goddess of the sword, strengthen our resolve.
  Goddess of the fiery arrow, help wrath find its target.
  Goddess of the law, let justice prevail.

  Goddess of music, strike a chord that will soothe us.
  Goddess of speech, bring words of comfort.
  Goddess of writing, inspire words of pride.
  Goddess of song, teach sweet lamentations.
  Goddess of poetry, give love a voice.

  Goddess of knowledge, assist with the search.
  Goddess of oracles, show us the way.
  Goddess of prophecy, help us see a new world.
  Goddess of rituals, fuel our candles of remembrance.
  Goddess of light, guide souls through the veil.

Goddess of domestic arts, protect our home.
Goddess of renewal, manifest unity and purpose.
Goddess of magic, transform our pain.
Goddess of healing, make us whole.
Goddess of invocation, hear our prayer.

So mote it be.

Names

Clay Gilbert

There is still power in the ancient names,
though we gather on the rooftop
of a high-rise apartment building,
and not at the summit of a great pyramid,
or in a circle of stones in the English countryside.

There is still power in the ancient names;
(Isis, Astarte, Diana)
the monuments of modernity fall away around us
as we sound them forth
(Hecate, Demeter, Kali);

These heights are a Witch's dream—
no flying ointment,
no faery wings
bear us skyward atop this concrete dolmen,
this urban surrogate for the Stonehenge monoliths.

No grove beneath our feet,
only the rough skin of gravel and concrete,
yet from beneath and from above
Earth and Moon shock us
into a revelation now complete—

Yeats was right, and H.D., and Pound:
There is still power in the ancient names,
(Hermes, Cernunnos, Osiris)
They still survive, whispered by the wind

that blows through gaps in weathered stones
(Odin, Anubis, Apollo)
that sings in lines conjured by the poet's wand,
that pierces airplane-scream and traffic-howl,
crowd-clamor and the choking cloud of smog.

This whisper-wind is our conspirator,
for she too has an old name,
Inspiration,
breath of divinity;

Forgotten, she does not die,
but sleeps, whispering in her dreams
(Dreams that are the lives of men)
until these words, remembered, wake her:

From stone circles to steel towers
in a disenchanted empire, this remains—
    there is still power in the ancient names.

4.

"Power and Compassion"

RITES OF PASSAGE

Birth, adulthood, parenthood, old age—one of the impulses behind Pagan rituals is to mark our life cycles, to take note and remember our endings and beginnings. In addition, these poems mark times that may not be as obvious, such as an initiation, or a passage from one set of attitudes to the next.

Being the Witch
Magdalena Alagna

I played the wicked witch of the west in Wizard of Oz,
In 8th grade, at Applegarth Junior High. Typecasting,
Everyone said, because I scowled in class pictures,
Because I had screaming bouts with my parents
Because I ate so little that my nose and chin grew sharp,
My fingers like twigs, my breath sour. A witch, they
        called me.

When I appeared onstage, green face, cone hat,
Pointy shoes, striped socks, black cape,

A baby in the first row began to bawl. I was enthralled
With the ability to wreak fear on others. I discovered
That power is its own gender. I was not just a skinny girl
With big boobs, who looked like a broomstick with tits.
I was what whispered amid the garments in a dark
     closet.

Not once had I wanted to be Dorothy with that awful
     getup—
Who wears sequined shoes with a gingham jumper?
I wanted to wear black garters and make boys suffer.
I wanted to sneak out at night, drink rum and coke and
Smoke cigarettes and wear too-red lipstick on my potty
     mouth.
I wanted to be left alone, to read Tarot cards, make juju
     bags
Bursting with herbs and rose quartz and melted wax. I
     wanted
To dance naked and chant in the woods the names of
     snake goddesses
I wanted to eat honey and apples and peanut butter I
     wanted to love
My body ripe and round I wanted to bang drums and
     spread my limbs and
Draw down the moon, paint runes on stones, conjure
     my blood's river and
Be what curls red in the night, be what blooms behind
     your eyes
When you close them in the bright sun, I wanted to be
     a witch and
Thank the goddess a witch, a stregha, is what I am.

The Black of Menopause

Judy Clark McCann

Walking through veil of menopause I look for friend
and understanding
but windows are few and far between
darkness remains unpierced by light for days or months
and dreams fragment into pictures of no meaning.

Drastic thoughts like arrows cut the bark of reality
scarring the surface of life without drawing sap
cloudy winter days are endless wrapping around the
sun, hiding insight
acting as courier for messages of stagnation

faces of those I used to know hold nothing but hurried
glances
shortened dances of hello and goodbye with not much
in between ketchup sandwiches

My body used to be friendly but now she turns into
someone foreign
that old woman on the screen with white bristles at her
mouth
and teeth yellow and broken into pieces of unspoken
communication

Sex and flirtation seem like cruel jokes of memory,
swats at flies that
always miss
Now grandmother's expressions echo in dreams
reminding me of parallels and parcels of information
from travelers beyond
Here holds little fascination now
the apples have shriveled on the trees looking forward
only to becoming seed
for the next generations

Black comforts me.

We Shared a Meal

Moushumi Chakrabarty

Outside, through the unquiet teeming skylanes
A puppet half moon roamed fitfully
Like a mad thing in search of meaning
A gay wind tripped in through the window
Giggling as my mother and I sat
Around the dining table, amid plates, glasses, spoons

With a helping of fat rice cooked white
My mother helped out that long-ago girl
With dreams in her eyes, hair tied up in ribboned plaits
Who sat on the chair's edge, and I heard with throbbing
    compassion
As she spoke about the red house of her birth,
Her earliest memories, her companions and dearest
Of them all, the little brother who died

Between the potatoes in the curry
My mother spied her adolescence, shy, nervous,
Unwilling to emerge, but wanting to
With a smile that felt old, I bore her out
Till she sat beside the others to speak with tender lips
Recount too, the tamarind taste of memories in the
Bamboo grove beside her father's house

Encouraged, they all emerged; chilly green bride and
    daughter-in-law
Fish curry mother with red sindoor* in her hair
Even the woman holding up her yellowed fingers
At the raining window to wash away years of cooking
    stains

We ate and drank with them, my mother and I
Till they slipped away like ghosts into our listening
    bodies.

*Sindoor: A red powder which Indian women use to line the parting of
their hair. It denotes marriage, fidelity and love for husband.

Handfasting

Julie Robertson

sacred, be the heart
that knows the In-Between
binds Spirit to Matter,
Mother to Father,
All to All,
me to you

sacred, be the heart
that sees Beyond
the scope of flesh,
through Distance,
through Time,
three thousand miles
your heart to mine

sacred, be the love
that passes in between
the ties that bind;
now and forever,
in you, there lies
the Immanent Divine

Thou art Goddess,
whose womb stands wide
gives life to all,
the shore of new beginning;
Thou art god,
whose seed makes fertile
barren lands,
who reaped the harvest
of the heart
with native hand

sacred, be the heart
sacred, be the love

sacred, be the heart
sacred, be the love

that knows the In-Between

The Dedicant

The Mystic Fool

"Go out and seek Divinity, my son," the High Priestess
    said.
"I shall," the neophyte stated boldly.
He shouldered his pack and sought a forest glade.
In the still of the night beneath the Blood Moon,
he removed four stones from his bundle.
Each was carved with an elemental symbol.
He placed the yellow air stone east,
the red fire stone south,
the blue water stone west,
and the green earth stone north.
Wand held high, he beckoned to the Goddess.
Athame to the sky, he called to the God.
His circle cast, he sat in the center.
The Dedicant whispered, "Deity, speak to me."
A wolf bayed.
But the boy did not hear.
So he yelled, "Deity, speak to me."
Thunder and lightning rolled across the sky.
But again, he did not listen.
The boy looked around and said, "Deity, let me see you."
A star shined brightly.
But he did not see.
The boy shouted, "Deity, show me a miracle."
In a tree a chick burst from its shell, a new life born.
But he did not notice.
So, the Dedicant cried out, "Touch me, Deity, and let
    me know you are here!"
Whereupon, Deity reached down and touched him.

But he brushed the butterfly away.
He solemnly stood and released the circle,
ending the ritual feeling despair.
"What did you find?" the High Priestess asked upon his
    return.
"Nothing, I'm afraid," he said, his eyes to the ground.
"Nonsense!" she replied, "You simply failed to notice."
"The Goddess spoke in the throat of the wolf,
the God through the thunder that roared in the sky.
The twinkling star was the God before you,
the birth of the chick the Goddess' own miracle.
And finally, the butterfly you shooed was the touch of
    the Gods!
You see my son, you must seek the Divine in all things
    great and small,
and you must expect the unexpected, to discover
    Divinity at all."

The Womb

Kay Jordan

I am a genie with more curses than wishes,
        Pandora spilling timeless tricks.
    I count childishly, capriciously, prizing
        inconvenience as much as regularity.
    I splash spheres of influence across her face
and swell internal seas along her belly's beach.
        I forge alliances with breast and thigh;
    I negotiate treaties with lip's tender lie.
    I blur the boundaries between plan and impulse,
            logic and desire,
            sense and sensuality.
        I rout reason. I conquer caution.

Once, twice, I raised my roof and expanded my walls
    to harbor hope, to house a love.

I was temple, palace, citadel,
antiquity alive.
But when love's labor left to lie upon her breast,
my walls wept with loneliness.
I echoed ruined emptiness and blighted
the tidy landscape
of her suburban body.
And now, now my glory days are gone.

Oh, I still play my youthful tricks and weave the ageless
spells,
but I am age entombed in middle age.
Soon I will be a craftless knitter
unraveled by the moon,
But I will remember the days when once, twice,
I embroidered fragile threads
onto the fabric of eternity.
And so will she.

Rite of Passage
Maureen Tolman Flannery

In the fullness of summer
when fluid surges upward in all things ripening,
and mischief flutters, hums
and finds its way through little cracks,
the boys, this rite of passage week
breathe in the lake till its murky green water
froths and sloshes through their entrails.

These boys have new noses that experiment with form,
trying to settle into manly features.
Their voices vacillate, and limbs,
like pulled taffy, elongate as we watch.
Disproportionately feet, they fling themselves
across furniture dwarfed by their gangliness,

leaving a stamp of damp
wherever they sit with dripping suits,
and trailing a wake of soggy towels
and sweat socks we veer around like skillful skiers.

The sequin night lures them into keeping her company.
They play basketball in moon-deserted water by the pier,
baseball around their damp floor mattresses,
anything but sleep with its warm, soft dreams
of flesh and triumph.

What goes on among them when they are alone?
After we have gone to bed,
do they paint themselves and
dance around the ceremonial fire?
Is the oldest first to fast,
isolate himself in woods,
dream of torrential rainfall,
his vision for the tribe to be read by the seer?
Do they cut ridges in his flesh
for entry of the blood of each?
Must he then stalk a stag and take it down
with an arrow he has worked from brittle flint?
As he smokes the pipe in the center of their circle
his pupils darken vertically.
He has become a mountain lion leaping crevasses
as paws of fur, like air set down on granite, quartz
find routes before unknown,
link cliffs to creek bed, span gullies,
ascend the peak. I see him stand
looking across pine spiked inclines,
revealing in his crimson cave stalactite teeth
past which a primal roar echoes through the canyon.

The next morning
I imagine that they greet us differently.
They seem content to play croquet
and practice driving into town.

They join us for a game of volleyball,
the juices in their limbs fermenting,
as we work to lubricate abrasive bone on bone.
Their vital coming on quickly defeats us.
We must play another round, too soon alone.

Time, like the male rabbit left too long in the cage
devours its young
till there is nothing of the litter
but its memory in the mind
of the mother rabbit.

Moon Flowers
Susan Clayton-Goldner

Balanced on the willowy branch
between girl and woman,
I boxed away that moonlit night,
two cane-seated rockers on the summer porch,
and my grandmother, a giant tortoise in her hands.
"He enters this world old," she whispered to me
or to no one, her pleated thumbs vanishing
into the parchment folds of his legs,
"And perhaps it is better that way."

After my grandfather died, she wallpapered
all the mirrors in her house.
Above the bathroom sink, two small mountains
of California Poppies hung.
Each night, as I brushed my teeth,
they waved their orange and yellow heads,
uncertain as I, in their newness.
She fastened Angel Trumpets and Fairybells
inside the twin mahogany ovals on her dresser.

And atop the mirrored tiles
Grandfather had hung to expand
the dining room, she pressed

an endless field of Alpine Forget-Me-Nots,
matched and smoothed their sapphire petals
with her long brush like a baby's hair,
the hair of my dead mother,
soft as the silken blue down
of a Hummingbird's throat.

Very slowly, as the weight of age
fell upon her, whitened her eyes
like the Night Blooming Cereus,
she awakened the silent nature of my heart.
And she knew someday I'd cross over,
unpack that night and remember
her, the tortoise and the moon,
how it hung, pasted and separate,
on the black sky like a mirror,
silver, and full.

To Sacrifice the Virgin
Jennifer Bradpiece

It was custom in Greece, the morning after
the night that turned sin to sacred:
Sheets displayed as proof of first possession,
Corner to corner tacked to wooden beams,
Crucified: Meaning drained like blood of a martyr.

She is nothing more than
an empty image:
Revered by
society,
an icon of the
civilized,
and obsolete by definition.

We stand up
for all that she
refuses to lie down for.

We swallow this
like children
starved for some
promise:
To be purified,
endeared to salvation.

We are taught
to worship
delusions of
man's grandeur.

It is the ritual
of savages—
Snow White on
her death bed,
Aurora in
her castle—
passive pearls,
inactive bones.

No matter
which divine law
man stutters
in his finest hour,
he always finds a way
to sacrifice the virgin:
Honor her with ceremony,
Create a spectacle
of her modesty.

She is his symbol,
raped by recognition,
fondled at the altar.

And if you pause
to consider
what the word meant,

at the time when
"hag" was wise woman
and "land" was not property,
when a "virgin" was a woman
of autonomy:
On her own,
loved as she desired,
and a number
not divisible.

For this renaming,
for this blasphemy,
no one was burned alive.
Instead,
it proved to be the perfect way
to sacrifice the virgin.

Shiva to Kali, on the Charnel Ground
Patricia Monaghan

Your lily feet! Your sweet red feet!
I feel them pounding on me,

pounding my chestbone, breaking
my heart in its case of bone,

breaking my bones, breaking my spine,
crushing me into rags and blood. Ecstasy.

Ecstasy. This is more than joy, this
moment of annihilation as you rip

out my heart and drink my blood,
as you cut off your head and throw it

to the wailing dogs. As your sweet feet
make music on my dying body, I open

everything I ever closed to you so
that you may leave nothing untouched

or undestroyed, I am not offering myself
for any other reason than to offer myself,

and because only as I am destroyed
will I finally know who I have been.

Kali to Shiva, on the Charnel Ground
Patricia Monaghan

The eye is a curious organ.
It blinks, and everything stops.
It blinks, and the world disappears.
You blinked.
I never stopped dancing.

The Crone
Darcie Callahan

She is an old woman working in a museum, dusting the
artifacts, adjusting corners. She preserves the past. She
saves history. She takes pride in her work.

She is a widow, and lives as widows do. There are times
when she is alone.

She dresses in black, and pulls her garments close about
her against the winter wind.

She takes in stray animals. She talks to them. She feeds
birds.

She is the silent supper, eaten alone.

She passes unnoticed on the street.

She is the strength of years. She is the weight of wisdom. She has forgotten more than you can remember. She remembers more than she can forget.

She is the grey of old hair, the dryness of old skin, the thinness of old bones, the timbre of old voice.

She places the roses on the gravestone, and picks off the wet, fallen leaves.

She is the calmness in the midst of depression, the dignity among sorrow. She knows loss, but she does not lose herself.

She is cobwebs and hot tea. She is dried herbs and small, grey mice. She is the clear faded blue of the winter morning sky.

She is an old cat slumbering on the hearth.

She listens to bad news quietly, not speaking. She nods her head as she takes in the words.

She is the ironic smile.

Think of her when the winter wind chills you. Think of her in the 3AM darkness. Think of her in the sadness and stillness. Think of her strength, and find it within you, for she is your ancestress, and her blood runs in your veins.

She has lived many times, and she lives again.

Think of her, and know you're not alone.

Persephone Speaks

Magdalena Alagna

When I had finally gone under
She halted all the earth's growing
Its wheat shrunk to sticks
Its onions to rinds
But she never noticed each day when I
Quenched myself at her side
Like a breeze holding its breath.

All she wanted was for me to watch her
Haul the grain into being; I had to
Stand at her right hand, whisper the litany
The peaches are great, mom, the roses too
And I am your most fabulous fruit
Dreaming of a knife to split me to the pith.

I wanted to be unmade of her making
I wanted to strip the bloom of me and
Purge the sap, tear my roots up and
Fling myself through the hateful ground
Of this world where every leaf, each
Blade of grass proclaimed her.

I managed it, too.
Did she think I wouldn't?
I leapt onto that chariot the way
A dandelion spur commends itself to wind.

Demeter's Grief

Magdalena Alagna

It wasn't when she left that day
Waving her arms in Hades' chariot
The daisy-chain she wore sliding askew.

What mother doesn't expect her
Child to be ripped from her side
The way she once was mined from her
Body's earth, cord cut?
What mother doesn't expect that?

It was how she separated from me
By degrees, bored and stalled in my
Warm, cinnamon kitchen.
She refused the fruit I coaxed
From the ground with my slow
Throat brimful of growing songs.
She started eating seaweed and tofu.

She roamed the field with a giggling
Gang of girls, picked wildflowers,
Savored the wounded, wilted bouquets
For days, holed up in her room
Pinned to the mirror, dissolving,
Problem-solving. She grew blurry,
Indistinct, until finally only
Twilight came to etch her on the
Bruise-colored sky.

Mornings found her tongue-tied
At the breakfast table, impatient
With my work, the charms that
Burgeoned the buds on their
Stems, that swelled the sap in the trees.

Once she had sat on my knee, begged
Mommy, sing the pinecone song,
Tell me again the charm that makes
The grasses come alive.

Then she couldn't wait to play outside.
She lay bent to the earth
Cheek pressed to the dirt as though
She could decipher the fire at its core.

No more little urchin hugging my
Skirts in the bright kitchen
Fascinated at how each seed
Burst its foment of bloom

Or stalk or vine. She was not mine
Not anymore. She wore eyeliner;
Her eyes like holes. Her nailpolish blue.
Her olive skin like a bone, bleaching

She tore up fistfuls of meadow grass
As she stood at a field's edge
Dredging her life and mine and
Finding the silt of rage. It's only her age

Everyone said but you know the story:
Grief pooled in my mouth, stunted my songs.
The earth sickened and wintered
When my little one, not so little, disappeared.

Before the torn slit of earth,
Before the chariot wheels greased
With sparks, before she was Queen

Of the underworld, Persephone's
Ripe mouth was mean and silent
As a snake in my kitchen and she
Awakened in stages over the
Orange tablecloth and fed my grief.

Counting My Feathers
Anthony Russell White

When the lightest part of me has floated free,
and someone has made a skimpy meal of my small
    weight,
only my scattered feathers will be left.

This large one to be a shaman's wand to ward off plague,
arbitrate property disputes, and show his authority,
these three in an ivory handle to fan a desert queen,
many more woven into a blanket to keep children warm,
others collected by young girls to dress their hair,
traded to neighbors to paint sacred designs on cave walls,
stuffed in rough pillows in a wood-cutter's hut,
dropped near doors by spies as coded signals,
clipped for writing pens to copy sacred texts,
ground to fine powder for herbal remedies,
scattered to cushion the wheels of a royal carriage,
picked up by a boy on his first day of walkabout,
bound to twigs as brushes to dust wooden altars,
others as decorations for war clubs, skirts for dancers,
earrings for brides, divination tools for necromancers,
rain cloak, chief's headdress, part of a new nest,
a little boy's ship in a rivulet after the storm,
a boy who wishes he could fly.

Beads

Gayle Brandeis

One by one, the women bring me beads—
Valarie, a stone, shaped smooth and white as bone;
Kathy, blue Israeli glass; my mother-in-law,
an amber bead her own mother wore.
It is my baby shower.
We sit in a circle like a string of pearls—
such shimmering women—
and they bring me beads . . .
from Cecilia and Jennifer, there are beads from Mexico—
one, amethyst quartz, 30 years old,
the other, glass swirled bright with color;
Kate gives a shell from a Baja beach,
Heather hands me a bottle-bead of Jitterbug Perfume.
Elisa's crystal has rainbows in its facets,

Margaret's Egyptian bangle shimmies like a belly dancer,
Whitney brings a piece of ancient bone.

We string the beads together, drape them around my neck.
The beads feel smooth and cool against my skin, solid;
they carry a weight stronger than glass and stone,
strong, the way breast milk comes out thin at first,
but grows richer with each pull of the baby's mouth;
strong, the way friendship grows richer
with each story we share.

One month later, the moon hanging in the sky
like a gleaming pendant, I put the necklace on.
In labor, I carry my friends with me,
my friends who have birthed and bled as women,
and they give me strength as they rest against my skin.
When my daughter is born through the circle of my body,
she is born into a circle of women,
a circle that welcomes her
just as the round, green, earth
welcomes the spring.

Samhain

Margaret McCarthy

When I was seven, I'd go looking for witches.
I didn't want to meet them   really
just glimpse them
because I knew that they were there,
their presence palpable in the raw October air
that smelled of apples and rotting wood.
I'd leave my mother's porch in my small shoes, coat
        buttoned
tight against all creation,
and I'd set out
to go looking for witches.

Under a blank sky I'd walk,
past the neighbors' houses, each with its jack-o-lantern,
seeds and strands of freshly emptied innards
clinging to carved out eyes and pulp teeth—
the dead aren't far away, they grin;
under a blank sky I'd walk, while the gray, lacteal light
drained from the day like milk from a cat's bowl.
Under a blank sky I'd walk, to the end of the block,
around the corner, to the end
of the known world—
as if by magic, all the neighbors' houses vanished, left
    behind,
and there it would be;
the lone spindly tree
or empty lot buried in dead leaves, that forbidden spot
where anything could happen.
Here, I'd think, *Here it is;*
this is where they live, I'm sure.

What child is not caught up with witches,
and the pain buried at the heart of everything?
The terrible hand of the unknown tugs on our coats,
        saying:
Find me; I won't be argued with.
The lure of the incomprehensible pulls like a tide
on a small boat, makes each child a true Celt,

sailing for the edge of the world, a world
that will eat you up alive and spit out your bones.
Come here, it says. *Don't be afraid;*
I'll eat your heart
right out of you.

Who can go there? Safely
grown, who among us can navigate the tides of loss in
        our small boat of
bones, glimpse
the unbearable marvelous
and come back?

Is it any wonder we always just miss
seeing the witch?
The dead aren't far away, she whispers;
It's your life.

Now I will navigate my small boat towards her far-off,
     unknown island;
when I reach that unlovable place where she lives,
the pain at the heart of everything,
I'll stop,
wait for her in her backyard.

Medical Student's Prayer
to the Goddess of Birth
Margaret Hammitt-McDonald (Moonheart)

Goddess of the ripening belly and of the swelling grain,
Of the greening Earth and the waxing springtime—
You know the saga of each grass-blade as it grows,
The sweet song of the melon growing heavy on its vine,
And you count the young of each rabbit in the field
And each mouse trembling under leaf.

Birth Goddess, Goddess of giving-to-the-light,
I dedicate myself to you
As birth companion, future midwife and obstetrician,
To respect and honor the sacrament
Of life-spark imbuing flesh for the first time.
I promise to protect this holy environment of birth,
To give my knowledge, skill and heart to the safety of
     parents and child,
To the creation of a sacred space for this new one's first
     entrance,
To honor the wishes of the parents for their child's
     introduction to the world.
I acknowledge that my knowledge, skills and heart
Are in the service of this new family,

Not my own interests, preoccupations or presumptions.
The birth-place is a place for awe, not arrogance.
I promise to intervene as little as possible
And to love as much as possible.

Mine are the first hands this new life will know.
Let them be filled with your spirit,
Your ever-expanding love,
Your wonder and delight in all newborn beings.
Let them welcome this new child with your light and
     love.

Let me always approach the birth-place with humility
     and respect.
Let me realize always that while I might assume,
The mother's body knows,
And it is to her I must listen.
Let me always trust my instincts and intuition
At least as much as my knowledge.
Let me be a friend and advocate for mother, father, child
     and family.

Goddess of Birth, my hands, my mind, and my heart are
     all yours.

5.

"To Me All Things Return"

POEMS OF GRIEF AND REMEMBRANCE

All faiths offer practitioners ways to understand and work through their losses, and rituals based on these human needs are often among the most powerful. Included here are poems of searing, personal grief, and also of more global grief, for the neglect of the gods or of the earth.

Heartstone
Patricia Wellingham-Jones

Mugwort (artemisia): said by Native Americans to induce dreams

Years after her husband died
she placed crushed mugwort in her left nostril,
stepped into the labyrinth, trod
the gravel path between lines of stone.
A few twists in, acorn rolling
between thumb and warm palm, she was surprised
to find her late love beside her deliberate steps.
The sun beat on her hatted head, the path

wound and wound and wound.
After several turns she stopped resisting,
felt him fill her body with tears
she'd thought long shed. Stunned
at an outer ring, her feet refused to move.
Amid rough lava and mica-chipped stone,
one not-too-large river cobble: smooth
and gray, inviting her fingers, with a heart
sunken in matrix of white. She felt her love
take her hand, lead her to the center. There,
in a rock hollow, she added the acorn to lichen,
cedar tip, faded flowers.
Expecting to feel calmed, she started
the outward trek, found tears spilling over
at the heartstone. With a sense of sacrilege,
she fished a tissue from her jeans and,
in one sharp blast, blew away tears—
and mugwort. A final pat of the stone,
a few steps further on gravel, her hair lifted
in the freshening breeze. She felt her husband's
smile rise over the oaks. Pace still deliberate,
heart and feet light, she stepped quickly
from the guidance of labyrinth
to the tangle of everyday.

Beloved, Hear Me
Galina Krasskova

I'm tired, Old Man.
I see no purpose in anything anymore.
Every breath has become a burden.
I wander through my days, a ghost of myself lost and
    alone.
I see nothing but years of bleak drudgery without
    comfort or surcease
stretching before me as the web stretches twined in
    the Tree.

I'm tired and so beyond hurt that I am numb.
What gifts you have given me turn to poison in my hands.
The vision of endless probabilities, endless threads,
the frenzied love of battle,
the constant, hawk like awareness of any inconsistency
      no matter how small,
the hair like trigger against inconstancy.
If I begged you to make the vision stop would you do so?
Would it make any difference at all?
Would I be anything at all without those gifts that
      torment my soul?
You hung for wisdom but what did You do for survival?
Every thread that connects me to feeling is slowly
      withering away.
I fear what it is I shall become, how alone I shall be.
What chance I had of learning to trust has been hung
      upon that hungry Tree.
It has made of me a thing of sharp edges, a weapon
      even in my own hand
with hurt its only will.
I have no more energy to scream or cry or rage, or love
      or hate or plead.
You know my weariness of heart. The grief of shattered
      thread upon shattered thread.
Make it quick, my Lover of Swift Battles.
Make it sure. Whatever remains of me at the end I give
      to You, Beloved.
If I am Yours then You also are mine.
And that is the only surety I can grasp in this darkness.

Diamonds

Maryanne Stahl

After-rain air is soft against my face, warm,
and oh my skin aches in gratitude and thirst.
Everything is grey and brown except
the lake, brown-green, a kind of ease against
the spastic wrench of muscle ripped from ribs.

I dream of my daughter dead, of keening,
of burial and unburying; fingerclaws of earth
unearth her—her face still beautiful—and
with mad, delicate turns unfasten diamonds
from her ears. I crave their light.

I say the words, "I have no daughter"
and I cannot breathe.

Before
Sonia Connolly

Can you hear it yet, murmuring inside?
I heard mine at two embryonic months,
And for ten long years after I politely
Declined teen-aged motherhood,
The small wild-eyed ghost followed after me
Babbling, reaching for his almost-Dad
Across three wide states, clutching at our hearts,
Binding us beyond betrayal with his longing.
We had to come together, finally, to say, "No."
Speaking into the black void of non-being,
With its bitter wind blowing on our faces.
No one much asks about life before birth.

After the Harvest Moon: A Wish
Marjorie Carlson Davis

If you could hear I would tell you
that fall is not the season of death;
that though tinged with brown
the plants are only dormant;
and that trees drop their multi-colored leaves
as a dog sheds its fur,
merely in preparation for winter.

If you could see the land now,
how sallow earth turns roseate
at the touch of a rising or setting sun,
how frost embraces the soil,
kisses the ground
with the soft white arms, cool lips
of a mother
sending her children to bed,
you would know life exists here still, only sleeping.

If you were free from the gasping
whir of this artificial lung,
I like to think of your spirit loosed,
your breath like a strong, fresh wind
whistling over these empty brown fields.

To Socrates, on the State of Philosophy in the Suburbs

Art Schwartz

Here in the suburbs, Socrates
in the courts of Crito's friends
there is a banquet every night
forgettable except for this,
we are less slender than before.

And as proof of this I offer my blank rolls
and unused ink, for as you know,
it is my habit to record those conversations
which, like cobbler's tools, might help us
in our own pursuit or craft.

These banquets end with sweets
and the emptiness left to the foolish lover
when Helius, awakening, must bear the sun
to new and favored places; Socrates,
one does no better here than guard against a loss.

Then in the morning, out beyond the wall,
these revelers are drawn to groves beside Illisus
where they make no sacrifice; their hope is for some
    shade
against the heat, and Simmias and I believe
the spirits have departed from this place.

Secrets Revealed, Our Un-Handfasting
Carrie Jankeloff-Edelstein

I wish I could say they were snipped one by one
Five ribbons cut
One motion

Love.
I see you lying on the bedroom floor
Your soft underbelly hanging out
And I am not permitted to touch
Or kiss or play or tickle like I used to
I still want to

Passion.
I brought you cups of hot black coffee
Your eyes still sleepy
We fucked transcendent into the sun
And you just barely out of dreamland

Trust.
Your shower faces
Teeth over lip
The way you struggled
Rather than ask for my help
Scrub the dirty spot on your back

Spirit.
That night
Self replaced by demons

Only your chanting brought me back
I love you
I love you
I love you
No mantra here to hold me now
I am lying awake for hours

Soul.
My regret for the nights
I asked you to trade your funk
For Classic Old Spice
Now find me nose to armpit
In a desperate inhalation
My last fix
At your last call

Body Parts
Dane Cervine

for Gaia, our earth-body

Another National Public Radio news report,
this time about the war in Bosnia, how the soldiers
left cardboard boxes boobytrapped
in the streets as they withdrew—
how the children would run
happily down the vacant streets
kicking over the boxes . . .

> *the nurses would gather the body parts
> so the mothers would have something
> to bury.*

Don't tell me about the world's secret symmetry.
I know the truth. Ask the sparrows
when they fall who holds their damp feathers,
the dew mixed with blood—except the earth,
ready to cradle all in her dark dirt breast.

Ask the mothers who cradle parts of their children
about the world's symmetry, about God's watchful eye.

I will tell you the truth. When Gaia discovered
what coming into being meant, uncovering
the dark that lurked in the creases and folds
of Her bright skirts, She shuddered and wept.
When Gaia pondered Her immensity
and could not stop it—could not halt the cruelty
in the light—She took form as a man, as a woman,
living in human fear and bliss again and again,
looking for Her budding children . . .

and dying not to forgive, but to ask forgiveness of us
for the cruelty we bear in Her birth . . .

> . . . and Gaia gathers Her body parts
> like a mother her children
> so we may find a way to bear
> this dark birthing towards the light.

Grief Prayer for Children
Yolanda Nieves

Goddess Tlazolteotl
protect my soul
I have died
not in childbirth
as you would have it
but in life
watching the children
of my flesh die
warriors wear their
skins on their
backs
no shroud can
convey my grief

my unfurled scroll
has no prayer request
breast milk runs dry
in my belly
I carry my dead
to Teotihuacan
there I will throw
myself into the fire
if only I could save
the grain.

Vigil

Sarah Brown Weitzman

The moon's half-eaten tonight
like the yellow apple
you wanted
but could not finish
in your last sickness.
I have come again
to clean the moss from the rocks
that guard you
from wolves, my son,
though I know your spirit is not here but climbs
among the silver web of stars
where you have the Dancing Bear
for a playmate and drink
from the Great Gourd
and perhaps forget us.
While your father sleeps
I come to do my work.
It is better
he does not know of this
He is resigned
about the moss
that thrives
while the corn withers

and that parents survive
their children.
Before he wakes
I must be back.
The moon will make false
day of my return
but I am afraid
the way will be dark, dark.

the phantom barn
Memory Peterson-Baur

The phantom barn remained there
longer than you would have thought,
and stood much straighter after
the great wind put an end to it.

Swallows in the empty air
circled and coasted, wings alert to snare
air currents rising from the vanished door,
to find the dim familiar maw once more.

A small black cat so suddenly had been
orphaned of refuge, after the wind began
the dance that snapped the old barn's spine in two,
it took her sense nine mornings to establish
that what her paws remembered wasn't true.

For days she called around the bare foundation,
until the wreckers broke that too,
and made a pit and bulldozed in the pieces,
shoving the monument inside the tomb—
    only roiled earth was left when they were through.

6.

"All Acts of Love and Pleasure"

POEMS OF PASSION

There are, of course, many forms of love and desire, and most Pagans are accepting of all that do not harm another. Here we find poems of passion and admiration, lust and friendship, love's beginnings and endings, and the interesting bits in between.

My Lover Gives the Five-Fold Kiss
Kiwi Carlisle

Was not where I'd expect to hear the words . . .
No neophyte was waiting for her name,
No circle stood, we'd not drawn down the moon.
Just two old lovers with their love made new
Brought out of time apart to come again
To find their love more beautiful and bright.
He sat right up and gave me a soft look
And lay across the bed in a new way.

"Blessed be the feet which have brought you in these
    paths."
I thank the night you reached for me again.

"Blessed be your knees which have knelt before the
    sacred altars."
My heart kneels at Her feet in grateful praise.

"Blessed be your womb, the source of all life."
All acts of love and pleasure sacred here . . .

"Blessed be your breasts, formed in strength and beauty."
And bless the touch which flowers them once more.

"Blessed be your lips, which have uttered the sacred
    names."
Venus, Astarte, Ishtar—hear my prayer.

The tears rolled down my face.
"What?" he said.
"It's beautiful."
"And so are you."
We slept a little then
And rested in the sacrament fulfilled.

To In Daghda, Summer 2001
Alexa Duir

There was a time, my Lord, my King, the stirrer of my
    loins,
When the world was cloven ruled, and then you came,
    and later, Lugh
And conquered us; I hated you. But all that changed,
    the day we two—

Ah well, you know that tale. The thing is all that
   changed:
When once our bodies met and joined, the past was
   disarranged.

It's hard to see you as they do, as others speak of you.
I do not know this King, and yet, there are echoes in
   the tales they spread
That do ring true of he with whom I choose to share my
   bed.

They talk of your enormous greed, and how your
   clothes don't fit,
Of your cauldron and your club, which split the skulls
   of men
And freed their souls, or else did knit their bones.

How absurd these stories are, my love, my Lord, the
   hastener of my breath,
As are the ones of me, as some dark harbinger of death.
(Does one create the thing one sees?) And now I am
   Goddess of crones
though still my form shouts out its sex, and all men
   want me; at my shrine
they find their secret pleasure—ah, but Dag—you ever
   did know mine.

On eves like this, 'neath Danu's swollen gaze, my mind
   turns back towards our days
And nights of passion, Ah, the fights we had! Our lust
   ran high;
Our bed was earth and sky, and fire ran through our
   veins, as still
It does 'neath my black Eye. Men like to think it's youth
   that gives the thrill
Which clothes true power. Ah, Dag, "These men are
   fools!" I hear you cry.
And they call you uncouth! But fools choose simple lies
   o'er complex truth.

They do not know you as I do, my Lord, my lover, and
      my friend. And those who spy
You now might well say there's less to you than meets
      the eye.
But how those poets loved to match your stature to
      your shadow, cast
At dawn. And yes, your cloaks were oft bedraggled and
      forlorn, but what of that? The man within was lusty,
      and of vast appetite (they got that right) for living,
      and greed to try to find the truth; to make amends,
      where due, but over all to never be in thrall to
      anyone, and to be true to friends.

They make of me a monster, and of you a figure of fun.
They talk as though our times are past, as though our
      day is done.
But while there is still pain and strife, and while there is
      a lust for life—
Then e'er so long I am your wife,
Your other half

The Morrigan

Night Returns to Her Lover, the Day
Tina Petrakis

Weary of holding the dying close,
Of dividing shadows,
I entered a garden of stone to rest.
And there, among those who lie as bones,
Those whose shades now weep
At the gates of Tartarus, at the ends
Of heaven, earth and sea,
I let my torch burn low.

But I glimpsed through my darkening sight
That even the frailest bud tethered at my feet

Opened its eyes in the dim phosphor;
That however small and misbegotten,
It felt the warmth of love.

I found my way home by the light of Hesperus,
In a world turned blue, draped
In brightness. And you were there,
Kneeling at my threshold,
Strong and golden, halo-haired,
Holding the orb of the Sun.

Cover me, my love, with light;
I hunger for your heat.
My gown is torn, my diadem has fallen —
    Kiss me now, before I sleep.

Red Candle

Maryanne Stahl

I wind a blood-red ribbon
round my hair; fasten small square
rubies to the roundness of my ears;
my shirt, a crimson pile, breasts bare
beneath,
against
the phantom coolness of your hands.

Speak to me.

You pull your collar up against
the teeth of winter air; steel
yourself, fortify, resolve
to catch the early train, and stare
sightless,
helpless
but for the rose petal caress your heart withstands.

Say my name.

The Holly's Song

Gizmo LittleWing

Down into the woods,
Where the wild holly grows,
Into thick green and strong,
The prickles warn the skin—
The way that they are,
And the way that I am,

Sister, calling.
Sister, I come

Where the bushes grow tall,
And triumph the life,
No tame or demureness
That holds back a passion
Of great joy in a winter,
Just joy in the being,

Sister, calling,
Sister, I come.

In a glade that's for shielding,
And lovers' hot games
And wild inhibition
I dance in the grove
Of the wild-ladies' making,
Their arms reach and scratch me
With reminders,
Sweet chides,

Sister, calling,
Sister, I come.

At the entrance, the gate
On the other side,
The back of the beauty,
A calm counterbalance

Of the fury and heat,
Stands the maiden-keeper.
She blushes for me.

For the way to my ladies
Is the tunnel of green,
Where voices laugh
And whispers lead on.
Temptation so right
That I have to dance it,
Have to call it,

Sister, I'm there.

A Bawdy Song
Kiwi Carlisle

Now Babylon is fallen, and the ziggurats no more
Stand in their dusty ranks against the sky.
All those long-vanished mud bricks turned the old
    Euphrates brown,
But Ishtar has a temple, a warm and living temple
Wherever Ishtar's priestess lays her down.

Nobody prays to Enki now and Nabu's but a name
All unknown to these chilly latter days.
Proud Ba'al, fabled lord of light, has lost all his renown,
But men cry out to Ishtar, sing praise to mighty Ishtar
Wherever Ishtar's priestess lays her down.

The bullock herds have all gone and the treasure house
    that bulged
With statuary, ingot, gem, and crown
Has lost its walls and ceiling to the gnawing tooth of time
But Ishtar takes her portion, her full and measured
    portion
Wherever Ishtar's priestess lays her down.

Now I have a reputation that some would blush to own;
They look askance at me all over town
And good wives stand and whisper, "She's a trollop, see
    that gown?"
But prayers ring out to Ishtar, all hail to blessed Ishtar
Wherever Ishtar's priestess lays her down.

So when I come to judgment where the gods sit in their
    halls
And prim and proper try to cast me down
Before me will rise a champion to save my soul for me
And Ishtar will preserve me though the Annunaki frown.
For Ishtar's had a temple, a happy, willing temple
Wherever Ishtar's priestess lays her down.

For the Unrequited

Sophie M. White

Like Horus,
He entered through a door of stone,
He exited through a door of iron.
He entered with his head down,
He exited with his feet down.
He found a maiden upon a spring of water.

However,
I desired, but he did not desire.
I agreed, but he did not agree.
I desired to love him
But he did not desire to receive my kiss.

I strengthened myself, I stood up.
I cried, I sighed
Until the tears from my eyes
Covered the soles of my feet.
Mother Isis, give me the words
To fill him with the fire.

Romancing the Crone

Dorothy Bates

My teakettle's a white swan, its long neck bends to my
    hand.
I twist dried flowers around a wreath of gnarled branches.
Outside, the earth sucks the milk of the Snow Queen.

At midnight, under goosedown, my body shivers,
shifts, returns to the form of 30 years ago.

Breasts become white doves nesting. Gray hair,
turned raven's wing, flies to my waist.
In the center of my heart, a harp begins to play.

He comes.

Ah, Krishna, Tammuz, Osiris—The Golden one is here.
Not body to body, but his body/my body/One body.
His hand/my hand, his voice/my voice.
The laser of his sex flows through me on rivers of light.

At dawn I wake to the sound of a silver flute.
Near my bed, a curved shadow—memento of the night
    gone by.
I pick it up and cradle it in my hand: one lock of
his black and shining hair.

The white swan spits hot tea. I choose my disguise with
    care:
dark coat, old scarf, black stockings, and such sensible
    shoes!
Taking the shape of an old woman, I go safely out,
into the sun's bright morning—into the world of the blind.

I am the Rose of Sharon and the Lily of the Valleys;
Queen of Heaven, Mother Goddess, Wise Woman,

Virgin   Mistress   Crone

Imbolc Eve

Jennifer Johnson

If you insist
that this Candlemas moon
was not born in the Bible,
she may think you quite mad
if you say it too soon, if you rush
into lamp-lit assertions
so easily had in bright carpeted rooms
in the middle of winter. And yet—

sweet spring simmers slowly
seeps into the skin
and will summon seduction
some clear night
some night soon
when a heavy white moon
hangs so low that you tangle your hair
in the full liquid light of the night.

Leave the bright lamps behind,
let wet grass be your carpet,
then say it. Let language suggest—
she will blush;
she will giggle
and slip off her shoes
in the lavender light
that turns frigid flesh fluid

and breaks through the ache
of a languid virginity.
She will blossom
like damp moss
on ancient trees
and the indigo shell of her sex
will then cradle the first
and the only religion.

Rescue

Corinne De Winter

Did you have to fall
In love
   Deeper
      Than where rests
The bones of travelers who never
Came back from winter
Voyages,
Where strings of pearls
And silver forks
And sea glass
Murmur together like
Old lovers,
Did you have to sink
As far as
   The wishing well's
End where pennies and
   Serpents and bloodworms
Commingle
In wicked changing symbols.
Did you have to fall
   Over and over
Through the air
   Like a scarlet leaf in November,
Divine and destined
   To dissolve against ice,
To tumble and spiral
Downward
Like the stricken acrobat
Who realizes too late
   That there is no
Greater risk
   Than diving
      For one's holy
         Beloved?

what did we do in the cornfield that night?
Deborah Dill

when you were married
I was not

when I was married
you were not

but in the cornfield that night

ah
I can not remember

I remember waltzing in the hayfield
          humming
            breathless
              twirling
      stumbling
in the dark of the moon

I remember the corn was higher than me
and you
and from the center
of the straight rowed field

no forward   no behind

only green sighs sprouting
from the soft earth

Aphrodite in Brooklyn

Lauren Raine

Please allow me to take off my shoes,
this faux marble pose
and this modern, pragmatic mask.
Permit me my ruin.

Let us not consider this therapy
or revolution
do not ask me to give you space
let us not discuss those who came before
and those who might follow.
Let us not talk of past lives.

I have fallen on hard times.
If you come to my temple
   just
    let me make for you an ocean.

Half seen in the darkness
your body, a mystery
true, tangible, radiant,
lined with the rings of your life.

You are beautiful,
beautiful to be a man.

Darling, even in this era, I will not believe
that love is disposable,
that sex is safe
that lovers are trains, rolling past each other
to some certain station

I remember,
I almost remember my river source
   My skin forms the word anew,
   yes,
   enter me
   as if you were coming home

Sappho Sings of Phaon on the Cliffs of Leucadia

Tina Petrakis

I.

They said it was a haughty love,
that I courted its baseness.
Perhaps I craved those wanton depths:
braided torrents that surge and rush,
one toward the other—
like you, once, toward me.

II.

Before I knew your embrace,
the smooth fit, taut and yielding,
I slept in dark, wet solitude and dreamed:
of our limbs, our lips, my hair undone
and falling across your chest,
our mingled scents of earth and sea;
I knelt in shallow waters
and wept—
a sigh's breadth from knowing
you'd bring that of the gods to me.

III.

How finely made! High-born
and sun-browned
with lips that shackled my heart
and left me warm—
even to my own touch.
So finely made! Headstrong, silent
and dressed for war;
eyes burning like bronze,
your full weight upon me
and I, your hard-won slave,
surrendered.

Free

Jennifer Schneider

Forgive me Goddess
for my playful
banter.
I am only a
virgin—
belonging to no man.
I wish for freedom
always.
They seem so much more
gentle
when I don't keep them near.
My strength is plenty
and I always
pick myself up
after a fall.
I take what I
need
and keep what I hold
dear.
Forever I wander
reaching for the stars.
I will find the one
in many men.
Laughing at their
fears.

Mirror, Me

Kathleen Landerman

Breathing in, I am
one with my shame.

Fear to look holds my whole body
immobile; my weight holds me
with more than gravity.

Breathing out, I am
my ugliness.

Vile, wretched, contemptible thing.
If the way is love,
then I should not speak these things
to myself.

Breathing in, I am my body.

If I gaze only at the reflection
of my pale belly,
then I will not see myself cry.

Breathing out, I am this image.

If I light candles,
and do not think of you,
then I can see a goddess
full of abundant harvests,
round, and smiling,
in my thighs.

Through the smoke of incense
these curves change,
become secrets,
invitations in velvet Braille.

If there was another woman here,
we could whisper the secret,
tell each other why a mirror
conquered the gorgon.

Breathing in, I am
no longer turned to stone
with shame, regret.

Breathing out, I am—
I am.

Fables
Marina Rubin

I once heard of a woman
who bakes cookies so delectable
that after one bite,
men fall in love, sobbing
and groveling at the hem of her dress
like delirious African cats.
Her secret is midnight and three
teaspoons of cinnamon and two
beads of menstrual blood
blended in a milky dough.

If suddenly I am tongue-tied
and stupefied beside you
on our idle celebrated street,
as if the moon collided with our balcony
and our cactuses and candlesticks
are landing on the pavement,
in this blast of sapphires and glass
if I clasp your wrist and crush your veins,
it's because I see curls of cinnamon linger ahead
and I hear oven doors slam.

pantoum for a witch's sabbath
Naomi Ruth Lowinsky

for leah

long ago when night was her familiar
she knew the moon and the moon knew her
i mean carnally
those stories about sex with the devil are about this

she knew the moon and the moon knew her
joy from the sky made a music in her body

those stories about sex with the devil are about this
moon penetration   stars awakening

joy from the sky made a music in her body
lion arose   horse flew
moon penetration   stars awakening
something from forever loved her for a night

lion arising   horse flying
roots of the tree reach up into the sky
something from forever loves her for a night
and the moon sings

roots of the tree reach up into the sky
branches touch down into earth
the moon sings
naked she is   and flying

branches touch down into earth
i mean carnally
naked she is   and flying
rooted in the night   her familiar

Augury

Marianne Wade

Am asked when I will remarry
as if the act is wholly mine.

As if I could run my hand
along the knobby spine of a man,
slide him from a shelf and say
you, you will be my husband.

Yours will be the mood lifted
by the rhythm of my voice,
your fear will be mine to eddy
and your joy mine to inhale.

In a wet curl of peelings,
spiral cut from a winter apple
by a mother who thought me beautiful,
yours was the name
spelled out in gauzy skin.

you, my horny god
Lee Carleton

throbbing pillar of joy
warm, welcoming holes
probing tongue of ecstasy
musky, pubic jungles
soft, gentle fingers
strong, massaging hands
excited nipples
deep, loving eyes
appreciative animal growls
happy laughter
cooperative climax
spurting, seeping holy fluids
spiritual oneness
through
sexual union
Pan is alive!

Taking the Earth as a Lover
Selchie

I lie with her
    stroke blades of grass
    with fingertips explore
        plantain stalk
        slender
        pebbled staff

          trace clover leaf
               small
               wet circles
               like aureoles

Feel where we connect
          supported by her body
          we breathe together
          we breathe together
                    pelvis pressing into earth
                    stone-cool against thigh
                    her body rising to meet mine

Face against turf, cheek soft on moss
          taking in her scent
                    sweet
                    green
                    earth-damp
          humus-rich I surrender to
Her ancient perfume
Enter her caves
          in darkness
          feel her moist in me
          In darkness feel her moist in me

Enveloped in her wetness
Enveloped in her warmth
          going deeper
          core deep
                    to heat
                    uh
                    hot breath
                    uh
                    shudder
                    spasm of release
                    from this body
Into Her.

A Picnic by the River with my Lover

E. W. Richardson

On a checkered blanket, in the shade of a tree,
I lay surrounded by the remains
of our picnic . . . fruits and cheese,
a sourdough loaf freshly baked,
and a rich red wine, not yet opened.
It is a fine day . . . a pale blue sky
filled with masses of white, puffy clouds . . .
a light, gusty breeze that swirls about . . .
Against this backdrop there is you,
playing at the river's edge.
The waters gurgle and lick around bare legs,
as you wade in the shallows,
dress hiked up to avoid getting wet,
the bareness of calves,
the flash of shadowed thighs stirs me . . .
The breeze plays games with your hair,
fluffing it up, blowing it across your face . . .
you push it back, but the mischievous wind
just pushes it back again, until
you end the game, and tie it up with a ribbon.
What a feast to the eye you are . . .
a wood nymph in communion with the Goddess,
a druidess in search of a rare, exotic herb . . .
and I, the awed mortal, helpless
before your charms.
I shake my head . . . a soft laugh,
and reach for the wine.
The cork pops free, and when I pour,
the sound of the wine, splashing into the glasses
mimics the river's song.
I call to you, holding up a glass
and you turn, smiling that special way,
that causes my heart to leap, my blood to heat.
Leaving your play, you step onto the grass,
the dress released, flowing about wet legs,

clinging here and there . . . and for one glorious
    moment . . .
the sun behind filters through the light dress you wear,
revealing your form in silhouette
the sky and water and dress . . . merely your corona
as you eclipse the sun.

A Sonnet of the Moon
Charles Best

Look how the pale queen of the silent night
Doth cause the ocean to attend upon her,
And he, as long as she is in his sight,
With her full tide is ready her to honor.
But when the silver waggon of the moon
Is mounted up so high he cannot follow,
The sea calls home his crystal waves to moan,
And with low ebb doth manifest his sorrow.
So you that are the sovereign of my heart
Have all my joys attending on your will;
My joys low-ebbing when you do depart,
When you return their tide my heart doth fill.
    So as you come and as you do depart,
    Joys ebb and flow within my tender heart.

Dionysus in the Curtains
Frank Miller

You were in the curtains that night, Dionysus.
I saw you—old voyeur, peering down at us with that
    sacred leer,
Measuring our fair limbs entwined.

Oh, I knew exactly why you were there,
Envious, yearning—a god trapped in muslin works his
    divine will
Upon young bodies.

"Imagination," she said afterwards,
"Faces in an inkblot—or perhaps the influence of wine.
You drink too much wine, you know."

Well, wine or not, I had my doubts then,
And, grown all these years older, I have them still.

Why, sometimes, summer nights, when the breeze blew
Through the curtains of our ancient apartment,
One glimpse of you naked in the shadows,

And I'd be irrevocably taken—
Fallen into soft arms, wholly obliterated in sense—
A divine trembling; that is to say, god-possessed.

Vine leaves in your hair, oh, Dionysus—
Old deviant father, incestuous friend and jealous rival—
I trust you were satisfied.

No Second Troy
William Butler Yeats

Why should I blame her that she filled my days
With misery, or that she would of late
Have taught to ignorant men most violent ways,
Or hurled the little streets upon the great,
Had they but courage equal to desire?
What could have made her peaceful with a mind
That nobleness made simple as a fire,
With beauty like a tightened bow, a kind
That is not natural in an age like this,
Being high and solitary and most stern?
Why, what could she have done being what she is?
    Was there another Troy for her to burn?

Her Face

Tim Harkins

She has a face.
The mother of us all. I saw it
in the moonlight, in our moment
of release, your head flung back,
your breasts arched, your thighs
wrapped tight around my hips.
Our moans rose like a hymn of praise.
I saw her kindle magic
in your eyes, saw her shimmer
along your silvered skin, heard the voice
that would answer my prayers.
When your mouth sought mine, I knew
the goddess loved me.

7.

"To Learn All Sorcery"

POEMS OF MAGIC

Magic is what most people associate with Paganism and particularly with its largest subgroup, Wicca. A magical act may be a prayer, a candle-lighting, a divination, or something more. These poems tell of magical acts and accidents, of the intentions behind them, and of the sometimes surprising results.

divination
Karen R. Porter

find a pattern then
access the pattern
in fine sand
or sweep
of ravens' wings
circling gulls
leaving the
richness of their feathers
how stones play out

old marrow bones
clacking
as they're thrown
notches carved
in subtle wood
hazel, birch &
holy oak
nervous aspens
whispering
numbers
& their songs
vibrating through the universe
words
tumbling from heaven
injected
in your brain
or drawn
with slow deliberation
from the
earth

Neighborhood Watch
Rena Yount

Excuse me.

There's an old man with a praying mantis on his hand
down by your willow tree. They seem to be smiling at
      each other.
I thought you should know. And by the pool in the park?
a woman with closed eyes is dancing barefoot in the grass,

upon which apple blossoms fall like scattered notes
in an unforeseen song. She's probably on drugs.
Or else it's a cult. A little girl is standing
in awe of the globe of golden light that swirls between
      her hands.

That's a cult thing, right? I think I read about it.
They teach these kids to think they're made of light,
or God, like Shirley MacLaine. Better call Protective
    Services,
before she swallows everything they say.
And opens like the dawn and flies away.

Types of Spook
Tony Grist

Ghosts are mainly sorry saps,
Unable to get out of here.
Maybe they died suddenly
And haven't yet worked out they're dead
Or maybe something holds them back:
Fear, greed or anxiety.
Madame Beswick's a good example.
Legend says that being afraid
The Highlanders would loot her house
When they came south in '45,
She buried pots of coin and jewels
Around her land and for some reason
Never dug them up again.
But after death she couldn't rest
And fretted for them something dreadful,
Scaring people with her pale
And dolorous face and playing tricks
Like lifting farmer Something's cow
Into his hayloft. Even though
They razed her house at Birchen Bower
And built a factory over it,
Night watchmen would catch sight of her
Flitting around.
But others seem
Not to be conscious. They'll show up
And patter through a fixed routine

That never varies—like the squad
Of travel-stained auxiliaries,
Led by a mounted officer,
Who pass along the Roman road
That's now a cellar floor in York.
It's like the stone's recorded them
And plays them back as video
Or—itself a living thing—
(And this is what I'd like to think)
Revolves them in its slow, slow mind.

Essense

Seabhacgheal

I strike a match, the head flares,
Incandescent, red to black,
As fire blossoms,
Struggling against its captivity.
I burn herbs in the old way:
Sage for cleansing and purity,
The pungent scent of sanctity;
Marigold and Lavender for the Fey;
Sandalwood and Solomon's Seal
(My charred offerings
Transmuted into scent and spirit);
Vesta Powder, because it cleanses
And because I love the way
It encourages the flames
To dance the colours of roses.
The smoke, sharp and heavy,
too full of itself, too aware
Of its own power, curls slowly out
Dispersing like dust, finely layered,
Pulling my prayers in its wake.

Fortune Telling in Southern Colorado

Candace Walworth

Libre, Colorado

A pinon pine catches my eye
sits me down & asks if I read
fortunes

Tracing the spirals, coils & crescents of her bark with
      my fingers
I surmise she will live a long, full life
before lightning strikes

You will give birth
to a baby pinon pine
who will beget hillsides of pinon pines

who will beget fishermen throwing lures
into lakes on distant shores

Every square inch of you
will be some creature's valentine

Before you go
touch me here she cries
pointing a gnarled finger to a clearing
in the sky

How to Be a Shaman 2

John Gilgun

Enter into the electric motor.
　　Flow toward the magnet.
　　　　Swim with the current in the wire.

Do not attempt to swim against the current.
　　Instead go with it. Now
　　　　you encounter the loop.

You did not anticipate this.
　　A downward force pulls you to the right
　　　　as an upward force pulls you to the left.

Here is the crystal city.
　　Here you have entered the holy city of Sharjah.
　　　　Here there are miniature paintings—

water color on ivory, oil on metal, manuscript illuminations.
　　You don't have time to contemplate them.
　　　　We must move along swiftly.

Continue until you reach the split ring.
　　Now the magnetic field reverses.
　　　　Now you fall with dizzying speed into

multiple coils from which it will be difficult to
　　extract yourself. You are weary, understandably.
　　　　And now you find yourself in a human heart.

And yes this is the superior vena cava
　　through which light breaks
　　　　and this is the atria, yes.

And this is a young river,
　　a fast flowing, high energy environment,
　　　　billowing like a curtain through canyon walls.

One to Grow On, for a New York City Bike Messenger
Annette Opalczynski

I forgot the extra candle
on your birthday cake,
one to grow on,
one to keep you safe.
So, I knock on wood,
throw pennies into fountains
and make wishes for you.
You laugh and threaten
to break mirrors
and feed black cats
when they come to your door.
You already live
like the lit fuse
on a stick of dynamite.
Weeks go by and
you don't call me.
I imagine you biking
in midtown traffic.
You wear a satanic grin
because I think
I've killed you.

Sibyl of Cumae
Natalie J. Case

eternity wrested from the gods
in a promise never kept
> *would it have been so bad . . . to have a god as your*
> *lover?*
bought with seduction
sweetly plied
> *though your heart was never in it*

oracle of Apollo's light
whispering hidden truths
in disfigured phrases
    even then you knew the truth, didn't you?
for those willing to approach
    were they always so afraid?
wasting into the Womb of life
selling wisdom
to kings
    you were a goddess even then you know
in enigmatic pages
scribbled delusions
of inspirational madness
    or did you just make it seem that way?
foretelling distant moments
and dreams to come
on leaves that the wind carried away
    I'll bet you planned it that way . . .
    watching from the darkness of your cave
while eternity conspired
against you
    what was it that made you change your mind?
without the gifts
of beauty
or pleasure
    he took those quite easily from you
withering the frailty
of your human body,
your human soul
    did you cry out for mercy in those moments you
                    were sane?
until even you,
once proud enough
to claim Apollo as your lover,
    though you never did . . . I can't imagine why
would beg any who could hear you
    can the children in Naples still hear your voice?
for the release
of death

Fortune

Marina Rubin

I haven't seen her for a long time,
maybe because it's winter
and she is hanging her sign Reading—5 dollars
somewhere on the wall in Miami.
But on that summer day, she was unusually quiet,
not waving to strangers, not welcoming tourists.
Three layers of her stomach were hanging from the tiny
    stool,
and bees were circling around her wet forehead
and grotesque beard.
I remember the moisture of my hand in hers
when she said a curse was keeping us apart.
She leaned towards me and whispered she could save me
if I gave her twenty dollars to put up two candles.
I suggested she buy 12 candles for 87 cents in Kmart.
Her angry gaze pierced through me.
So I bought love and luck for 20 dollars and ran away
frightened that she would put another curse on us,
in addition to the one we already had.

The Bird Oracles

Patricia Monaghan

Gray sparrow, dead, in front of a door:
    Do not hold yourself aloof from what is coming.
    Suspense and fulfillment, complete emptiness.
    Embrace strange animals for the full answer.

Seagull at noon, crying louder than bells:
    Who comes now will be blessed and burdened.
    Serving and commanding: one and the same.
    Dreams will not matter, only omens.

Mourning doves, nesting above a door:
> Every thread is part of the inevitable design.
> Weeping and consoling, the same sound.
> It will fall. It is only a matter of when.

Falcon, like a guardian of the circle:
> Even simple things grow complicated at the end.
> A beak like a knife. An eye like a knife.
> Lie on a volcano's rim and look down.

Raven, on a chair, screaming:
> You have come home. Come home.
> Underfoot, fragrances and poisons.
> From blue distances, the sound of rain.

Owl, just before dawn, in the street:
> Who goes now was never really here.
> Light and shadow, a matter of position.
> What is the only direction a song can move?

The Candle

JoAnn Anglin

Only has value when it is consumed
Is only alive when it shines in the dark

Is a meaningless thing
Until married to flame

Depends on another light for its own light
Throws light, throws shadow
Shows the silhouette dark by sharing the light

Shows the possible beauty—the edge of the solid
Shows the danger and hints at safety
But shows nothing beyond.

Shifts the shape of the space it lives in
Lives in the shape of the space it makes

Dances in breezes, reflects breath of life
Illuminates but never completely
Echoes the past as it glows ahead

Pulls our history into our hearts
We are with those who lighted
Candles before us, and those before them
And to timeless before.

Nourishment
Loralee Clark

My sacrum bloats and swells with pain as I get the flour
down from the shelf. Bending to reach into the
    refrigerator;
my lower back smiles relief.

I test the water, wait until it is blood-ready before I bless
    it with the yeast and honey.
I lie on my back and hum softly while it grows,
feeding on the heat and sweetness.
Yeast colonies multiply as the flour resigns itself to the
    gravity of the bowl.

Eventually I stand, inhaling the yeasty froth,
pouring it into the flour well, tossing handfuls of the
    softness
into liquid. As I mix the stickiness folds into itself.
As I knead, the two become rubbery, dense. As it rises,
I collect this moon's blood,
this cycle which separates me from other animals,
this ancient knowing encoded in my cells.

I punch the growing dough down and fold my moon's
    blood
into the batter.
It stays brown with a pocket of red
then it melts into pink, encompassing all of the dough.
This is the sun dying into the sky, relinquishing day.
This is the fallen petals of a rose.

I turn this sacred tissue into food for the earth;
I make this bread to give back to her.
This blood
which will never nourish a growing child
shall be an offering for other life.

After the dough has risen again, I place it in an oven of
    clay.
Let it cook inside and out. Let it cool.
And in the dusk of evening with the moon full overhead,
I dig a hole deep in my garden between the tomatoes
    and dill.
I place this dark loaf into the ground and pray for health.
I honor the cycles of the earth, the cycles of woman and
the blood which feeds life. And so,
I feed the heart.

I Became

Anna Mills

In sixteen summers in the high country,
it happened once.
I was trekking over ground squirrel tunnels
between white boulders and a meadow sloping to the
    river,
breathing thin air,
watching for arrowheads and fat marmots,
sun beating on my neck and on the frail earth, melting
    its snow covering.

I became a lioness.

A surge of yellow song in my blood.
A light and infinite step
over birthland, sleepingland, drinkingland.

I had always been what I was:
striding over the grass
tireless, buzzing with light.
My eyes swept over a thick granite peak,
a lake hidden in a pocket like a hanging basket,
a stream snaking through the willow,
making waterfalls over jagged rock.

*The earth is mine
and I am the earth's.*

My companion noticed nothing
except my humming,
swelling and fading with the secret.

Shapechanger
Eileen Malone

He forces a kiss, claims her
closes his eyes as she slips and oozes
from a manifesting giant snail shell

secretes a path behind her
pretends to cherish his longing
for unknown chambers indicating
an entrance for him cleared of slime

muffles his demands with her mouth
as the rest of her re-enters backwards
her brittle self

and he thinks he receives it
like a smug winner in a grown-up game

and as the controlled and overpowered
she yields

lets him slurp and suck into his mouth
what he sooner or later
will abruptly recognize
as a most peculiar
cold and snail-gray tongue.

Ann

Robert Lord Keyes

She's a psychologist
comes to the circle
has to take it off
like we all do
says she doesn't see
clients this way
but takes part
in the readings,
in the passing of the
chalice and athame
like moth to a flame,
even gets to crown
the Oak King with thorns
later has a beer with us
at Cold Spring Pizza
taking notes in her head
all the time as we
laugh, joke, and carry on
says she wished
her profession were
as direct as this

and yet has begun
unconsciously casting her
first magic spell
to the winds

The Magician's Card
CB Follett

I raise my candle lit at both ends,
although the space around me is filled
with a yellow solid as steel.
The candle points both up toward the sun

waning, down toward the moon waxing,
and my other hand points to Earth
where the lilies of Easter
and roses of resurrection, open at my feet.

Before me the table, the cup, the pentagram.
There is white magic here, serene
though I appear, I can change things
in the wink of a star.

I can turn Earth on its axis from day
into night and back again, before
you have time to sort your mind into clarity.
My feet, buried in flowers, have a path

they will not show you. What you think
you see, you have not seen. What you know
is riddled as a sieve. I am the alpha
and omega, the penultimate, the ultimate.

Over my head, the eternal rope.
Over my head, the I of the ego,
that trickster who can make you dance a jig
strange and delusional.

*   *

Sit beside me, draw your knees
under the planks I nailed myself.
I wear the white of purity and the cloak
of forgetting. What you ask of me is flawed.

I change water into wine, it was what you wanted
but now, what will you do without water?
How will you feed your skin and the discs of your back,
now you have chosen the grape over the well,

grapes plucked and pressed, the well
boarded over. You hold up your hand to me,
looking for miracles. Look within. I am
but a puppet of the sleight of the eye.

You have given me the power.
With my light and my left hand
I consign you. The flowers
you think to smell are only paper.

For a Friend Lying in Intensive Care, Waiting for Her White Blood Cells to Rejuvenate After a Bone Marrow Transplant

Barbara Crooker

for Judy

The jonquils. They come back. They split the earth with
    their green swords, bearing cups of light.
The forsythia comes back, spraying its thin whips with
    blossom, one loud yellow shout.
The robins. They come back. They pull the sun on the
    silver thread of their song.
The iris come back. They dance in the soft air in silken
    gowns of midnight blue.

The lilacs come back. They trail their perfume like a
    scarf of violet chiffon.
And the leaves come back, on every tree and bush,
    millions and millions of small green hands
    applauding your return.

The Sacrifice

C. Leigh McGinley

My tabby cat
Is ensuring our survival,
Bringing sacrifices of small rodents
From the garden.
No morsel for his appetite,
He places them reverently
On the stone in the ancient way,
Where the sun dries them and the ants
Take them away bit by bit,
Leaving only bleached bones
And a smattering of fur.
He knows, my tabby,
That, for all my enlightenment,
I have forgotten
That the cosmos must be renewed,
And I wonder sometimes
If, by the diligence of my tabby,
Rodents will someday
Replace us in the world.

8.

"Mirth and Reverence"

POEMS OF LAUGHTER

Who says all poetry has to be somber and significant? Laughter is healthy and necessary, and when used appropriately in ritual, it can bring people together in a memorable and joyous moment. These poems celebrate the funny side of Paganism and of life.

A Charm Against Love Charms, or Breaking Up with a Witch
Andrew Nicoll

Go out in the woods
Butt naked from your head to your boots
Dance round in a ring
shout and sing
Light your candles, shake your bones, brew your roots
You won't make me love you
And you won't know why.
You got relics, you got Tarot
You got a quill from Cupid's arrow

You got enough wax dolls to fill a barrow
You won't make me love you
And you won't know why
I get up in the morning and you're in my head
I lie down at night and you're in my bed
I see you naked, or you're in lace
I can smell you, I can touch you and I kiss your face
And there's things I do to that secret place
But you won't make me love you
And you won't know why
I get crazy, I get mad
I want you so much and I need you so bad
Above all else, I'm more than sad
But you won't make me love you
And you won't know why
So you can spell your spells
And you can hex your hex
The girls in the coven can place their bets
And the more that I'm without you, the worse it gets
But you won't make me love you
And you won't know why.

How My Hair Caught Fire in My First-Ever Ritual and Ignited the Spark of My Mother's Never-Yet-Relieved Doubts About My Spiritual Path

MaryJane Millington

Sixteen with a jones
for the Pre-Raphaelites,
two red tapers for love
and a butane kitchen lighter;
wax melts down past
his carved-in initials
and my head is bowed
to my minted goddess.

I never knew that magic
would smell funny
shifts from a passing thought
to a wet reality
as my mother,
extinguisher in her hand
and incredulity in her eye,
douses my first attempt
at a new religion.

Gertrude, the Goddess of Abandon

Cher Holt-Fortin

"See that one," Gertrude sidles up to me,
waving beringed finger.
"My Thanksgiving turkey never had such a perfect
    brown."
She's right of course, the woman in question
has crisp brown skin.

"But," I say, "the electric green bikini sets it off so well."

I on vacation,
avoiding growing old,
on the beach of eternal youth.

"So how come," says Gertrude, nodding toward
a man whose stomach obscures his bikini,
"how come you Yankees come in two kinds?
I mean look at those Canadians, lobsters."
She laughs. "And that one, he's been a beach
bum since the '60s."

"And he looks it," I say.

She pokes me familiarly,
with a long red nail

that matches her own bikini and high-heeled jellies.
Gertrude is Rubenesque, a look I envy,
but can't let myself go to.
"And then," she pokes me again. "There is you."

I resent the poking, but she is the goddess.
"Me?" I ask, admiring a tern.

"Look at you! You're wearing shorts,
and a long sleeve shirt."
The shorts reach my knees and I have on a hat.

"Sun causes skin cancer," I say,
but I mean it causes wrinkles.

I sidle a little further into the water.
"I have a bathing suit on under."
Not that I intend to use it.

"So," she snorts. "Despite
all my invitations, you won't take off your clothes."

I look again at
women browned to a crisp,
and the wintering Canadians,
so pink and lovely in
their new sunburns.
The goddess of abandon
reigns among her palm trees and seagulls,
neon votary candles everywhere.
Voluptuous, carnal,
so unlike Athena, the goddess I know best.

Gertrude scoffs at Athena, "Balance? Wisdom?
Temperance," she laughs.

"Abandon such clothes, such corsets,"
her palms whisper.
"Be free," her gulls call.

The sun melts me
And I undress, oil and prostrate
myself in the sun, crawl into those maternal
waters to be undone, freed.

for Clare
M. P. Mann

Once upon a time,
her golden ball slipped under the water.
She cried, made a bargain with a frog,
took her ball, and went home.

What's wrong with this picture?
those words, the pictures
show a little girl, ten maybe, eleven
now think of it—

You sit by the pool
a frog speaks, bargains, brings
the golden ball
What do you do?

I would never have left.
Finally, at the very moment magic
enters my life, to leave?
No, I would stay, gazing,

conversing with this marvelous
green slippery wet thing
What could he not tell
of cool depths, of hidden springs?

Later, called home reluctantly to dine
the frog is in my pocket
green fingers splayed to lift
the arc of nose and mouth to the air

Commanded to wash off the slime
defiantly I place the frog at my plate
offer him whatever he wants
a bite of hamburger, a french fry

I keep him in my room, sure,
he's in my bed. At that age,
I'd kiss a magic frog
over a boy, any day.

Pan in Vermont
Rudyard Kipling

(About the 15th of this month you may expect our
Mr. ———, with the usual Spring Seed, etc., Catalogues.
—Florists' Announcement.)

It's forty in the shade to-day the spouting eaves declare;
The boulders nose above the drift, the southern slopes
    are bare;
Hub-deep in slush Apollo's car swings north along the
    Zodiac.
Good lack, the Spring is back, and Pan is on the road!

His house is Gee & Tellus' Sons,—so goes his jest with
    men—
He sold us Zeus knows what last year; he'll take us in
    again.
Disguised behind a livery-team, fur-coated, rubber-shod—
Yet Apis from the bull-pen lows—he knows his brother
    God!

Now down the lines of tasselled pines the yearning
    whispers wake
—Pitys of old thy love behold. Come in for Hermes' sake!

How long since that so-Boston boot with reeling Maenads
    ran?
Numen adest! Let be the rest. Pipe and we pay, O Pan.

(What though his phlox and hollyhocks ere half a month
    demised?
What though his ampelopsis clambered not as advertised?
Though every seed was guaranteed and every standard
    true—
Forget, forgive they did not live! Believe, and buy anew!)

Now o'er a careless knee he flings the painted page
    abroad—
Such bloom hath never eye beheld this side the Eden
    Sword;
Such fruit Pomona marks her own, yea, Liber oversees
That we may reach (one dollar each) the Lost Hesperides!

Serene, assenting, unabashed, he writes our orders down:—
Blue Asphodel on all our paths—a few true bays for
    crown—
Uncankered bud, immortal flower, and leaves that never
    fall—
Apples of Gold, of Youth, of Health—and—thank you,
    Pan, that's all.

He's off along the drifted pent to catch the Windsor train,
And swindle every citizen from Keene to Lake Champlain;
But where his goat's-hoof cut the crust—beloved, look
    below—
He's left us (I'll forgive him all) the may-flower 'neath her
    snow!

Worshiping Gods

Fred and Leigh
(with a little help from their friends)

(Tune: "Waltzing with Bears")

My Uncle Walter's been worshiping Gods
It's a god-awful thing that defies all the odds.
Every night in his room he reads "Calvin and Hobbes,"
Then he turns out the light and he worships the Gods.

> *Refrain:*
> Yes, he wor-, wor-, wor-, wor-, wor-, worships the
>   Gods;
> Ancient Gods, Pagan Gods, Goddesses too!
> There's nothing on earth Uncle Walter won't do,
> So he can go worship, wor-, wor-, wor-, worship,
> So he can go worship, worship the Gods.

I snuck in his room in the middle of the night,
Crept up to the door and I turned on the light,
But to my dismay, he was nowhere in sight!
I'm afraid Uncle Walter worships at night!

I gave him a bathrobe so he could relax,
But lately I've noticed it's covered with wax,
And there in the pockets, two new Tarot packs!
And sewn in the lining are strange little sacks!

We told Uncle Walter that he should be good,
And worship the way Falwell says that he should,
But I fear that he'd rather be out in the woods,
We're afraid that we've lost Uncle Walter for good!

We begged and we pleaded, "Oh, please won't you stay?"
And tried to take him to church for a day,
But the Goddess arrived and She held us at bay,
Now he worships Innanna, Diana and Gaia; he's trying
    to worship a Goddess each day!

We asked Uncle Walter just how does it feel,
To be one with the Gods, and to learn how to heal?
And he said, "Let's just see what the Goddess reveals,
When we go to Sabbat and help turn the wheel!"

That night when the moon rose, we crept out the back,
He took me to Circle where I'd learn the facts,
When the Goddess appeared, She told me, "Welcome
    back!"
Now it feels like flying, there is no denying, and now
    my bathrobe is all covered with wax.

My Aunt Matilda's as mad as can be,
"Walter, that rat, never invited me!"
So she took her bathrobe and she fixed it just right,
So she can go with us to worship at night!

At new moon and full, and sometimes in between,
Walter, it seems, is nowhere to be seen!
He's not off in the ether, nor has he gone between!
He's out in the woods with our new May Queen!

angels on the fly
Will Killhour

when it comes to hunting and fishing vagaries
I consult my neighbor
he's got all his reloading equipment
in the kitchen and a young wife
who lets him keep it there   she gives
us pine straw   she has tattoos

that boy next door   he says
it's open season on mythological creatures
the state legislature thinks
they're part of the dreaded New Age
and the Fish and Game officers refuse

to count or tag things that they don't
believe in and which could be Catholic

you can mostly get them at night
but you got to be ready   he says
they don't come in on a low angle
or glide like ducks or geese
when they come down to light on my roof
it's straight down
like they're falling out of the sky

they don't bounce   he goes on
you got to hit them just right
if you just take off one wing   they can
do some damage if they fall in his
truck patch   that one floppy wing
spins them   pathetic sight
for the sensitive   the head shot
gives him pause   he says

they are so light when they land
my lover doesn't wake
but I am up   ears tuned
for a divine word
that never comes
but our neighbor brings us fruit juicy
tomatoes and long crisp zucchini
my lover can cook   and it is
out of this world   heaven on earth

9.

"Dance, Sing, Feast"

CHANTS AND SONGS

These poems are meant to be heard rather than read. They are meant to leap off the page into sound, perhaps repeated in an energy-building chant or sung in a circle of friends. This is only a tiny sampling, meant to give some ideas of the way poetry can gain spiritual power through sound.

Grandmother's Song
Susan Landon

Great is the one
who bears the world
upon her shoulders,
spins the stars
in the sky.
Great is she
whose lightning bolt
pierces the heart
of darkness.

Musical Collect (to open circle)
Rita Moran

With the earth beneath our feet,
With the sky that shelters all,
With the breath that is our life,
With the fire in our hearts,
In this place of love and magic
Here we stand as one.

Protection
Bethanie Frank

Protected by nature
There are great powers
I invoke them to assist in my day.
Guide me
Protect me
The trees are my leaders
The field is my bed
Surround by that which I came
Unto the Earth is where I'll return.

Dancing Together
Eileen Blacklock

Tap a rhythm on the ground
Diana, Isis, call her name
See her in the candle flame
Incense burning, smell the flower
Try to raise a cone of power
Candles in the quarters flicker
Feet now stamping, going quicker
Fire burns and smoke is swirling
People dancing, people whirling

Dervishes, we move so fast
Ghostly echo of things past
Begin the chant, hypnotic drone
Maiden, Mother and the Crone
Glowing blue light start to build
Power growing as we willed
Feet now spinning on the ground
Hear earth's heartbeat as they pound
Voices chanting, high notes, low
With wonder, feel the power grow
Together with one mind and will
Spells and workings to fulfill
Eyes wide open, now we see
The spell is cast, so mote it be!

Thirsty Earth
Carre Jankeloff

Mother . . .
We watched the snow melt
We tilled the earth
Weeded
Planted seeds
And watched as they sprouted delicate buds
But mother, our earth goddess
We need rain
Your earth, our earth, is drying out
Owns an unquenchable thirst
So do our seeds
So do we
So here mother,
Brave and strong mother
We give you rice
Thrown into the air
Watch how it falls
Like heavy raindrops
Back to earth

For you we set cotton afire
To remind you how dry our throats are
How dry you must feel
So please
Give us rain
Put out the fire that has begun
Without you it will burn out of control
We need rain . . .

Rain for the trees
So mote it be
Rain for we
So mote it be

Rain for the trees
So mote it be
Rain for we
So mote it be . . .

Healing Chant
Burrowing Owl

Heal.
Heal.
Heal.

Heal my Body,
Heal my Spirit,
Heal my Flesh,
Heal my Soul.

Hear the voice,
Of one who follows,
Hear my Voice,
Make me Whole.

Oh Divine,
Oh Heart,
Oh Mother,
Hear my Cry.

Grant Thy Child,
Thy Silver Blessing,
Grant Thy Wings,
And Let me Fly.

Heal.
Heal.
Heal.

Branch and Bone

Rita Moran

Chorus:
I am the wise man; I am the fool;
I am the hunter and I am the kill.
I am the root that shatters stone,
And though I wane, I am with you still.

Of branch and bone, I build the world
With steady fire, I give the moon her light.
With passion proud I fill your heart
I am the God of nature's might.

Of standing stones on sacred ground,
They built a ring to mark my flight.
With priest and priestess they did dance
To celebrate the Lord of Light

In forest dark and secret grove,
In antlered dance I take my delight.
With cloven hooves I mark the earth,
With wild song, I pierce the night.

Goddess Invocation (in the city)

Beau Williamson

"Oh Mother I can feel your heart beat
even through this cold concrete."
—chant after invocation, learned from a California eco-activist.

Rejoice in the decay,m for she is in the weeds and the
  rust that reclaim the works of our hands.
  Goddess of Autumn, Goddess of the storehouse of
   all potential:
  Yours the heat that cracks
  Yours the water that erodes
  Yours the icy breath that chips away
  Yours the dust to which our work falls
   And from which we may build again.
 You give us the power to create
 Without you, no motion, no return;
 You give us the power to create
 We honour you and welcome you into our circle.

"MANY NAMES"
CONTRIBUTORS

Nilanshu Agrawal is a lecturer in English at a college in India, and a translator of English and Hindi texts. His poems have been published in American and English magazines.

Magdalena Alagna is a freelance writer and an editor at *Long Shot* magazine. She has performed and published extensively in New York City and its environs.

JoAnn Anglin's varied publishing history includes *The Sacramento Anthology: 100 Poems*. A poet-teacher at Shriners Hospital for Children, she has read her poetry at many venues.

Leondra Apollonaris has been practicing the Craft for seventeen years. She currently resides in Maryland with her partner.

Archer lives in Toronto with David, Neil, and Angie. Her current projects include a series of fantasy novels and a collection of Greek myths.

Barbara Ardinger of Long Beach, California, is the author of *Goddess Meditations, Practicing the Presence of the Goddess,* and the forthcoming *Finding New Goddesses: Reclaiming Playfulness in Our Spiritual Lives.*

Barbara Arnold is an educator, a Reiki practitioner, a priestess, a poet, the architect of her own spiritual path, an interfaith minister in training, a wife, a gardener, a pet owner, and a New Yorker.

Elizabeth Barrette is a well-known columnist and reviewer for Pagan publications.

Dorothy Bates is an editor, researcher, lyricist, and writer of special material for cabaret performers. She began writing poetry in 1995 and has been published in print and online.

Ellen Benson grew up in a literature-nurturing environment with a library of mythology, art, and psychology, learning how to dissect fables, unearthing their life lessons.

Michael E. Bérubé is a professional photographer living and working in western Maine. His poetry arises from his work on a spiritual path of Bardic Druidry.

Charles Best (fl. C.1602) was a Renaissance poet, now little known. "A Sonnet to the Moon" is his only surviving sonnet.

Eileen Blacklock, a member of the Pagan Federation, has had poems published regularly in its district magazines. She lives in Surrey on weekdays and Devon, weekends.

Jennifer Bradpiece is a student of creative writing and an intern at a literary arts center in Venice, California. Her poetry is inspired by pre-patriarchal cultures and ancient mythology.

Gayle Brandeis is the author of *FRUITFLESH: Seeds of Inspiration for Women Who Write*. She lives in Riverside, California, with her husband and two children.

Paul Brucker, a marketing communications writer, lives among the alligators of Mount Prospect, Illinois (where, officially, "friendliness is a way of life").

Geraldine Moorkens Byrne, a former advertising professional, works in her family's musical-instrument business and publishes the *Pagan Poetry Pages* ezine from her home in Dublin, Ireland.

Darcie Callahan wrote articles, stories, and poems for Pagan magazines in the late 1980s and early 1990s. "The Crone" is published for the first time in this anthology.

Lee Carleton is a college English professor and freelance writer from Richmond, Virginia, who celebrates the power and joy of happy sexual union in the face of our often repressive and frightening world.

Kiwi Carlisle has been an eclectic pagan, with a special devotion to Ishtar, since 1980. She lives in St. Louis and is a member of the Ozark Avalon Church of Nature.

Natalie J. Case is a thirty something poetess and shaman currently living in northern California. She has been writing poetry since she was fourteen, with varying degrees of success.

Dane Cervine lives in Santa Cruz, California, with his wife and two children. He has been published in several publications, and serves as chief of children's mental health for the county of Santa Cruz.

Moushumi Chakrabarty is a poet/writer based in Ontario, Canada, who says, "Reading a poem is for me like candy for my soul."

Loralee Clark teaches speech communication at the College of William and Mary and lives in Williamsburg, Virginia. She has recently been published in *The Cape Rock, Potpourri, Grasslands Review,* and *Sierra Nevada College Review.*

Susan Clayton-Goldner has published two novels and has appeared in many anthologies and journals. She lives on a horse farm in Tennessee and writes to avoid shoveling stalls.

SuzAnne C. Cole, a former college English instructor, is the author of *To Our Heart's Content: Meditations for Women Turning 50*, along with numerous essays, poems, short stories, and plays.

Sonia Connolly is a healer, Pagan, and poet dedicated to Kuan Yin and also drawn to the Greek pantheon.

Ellen Cooney studied magic with Starhawk and Diane di Prima during the '80s. She has published six poetry books with Duir Press.

Sandy Crimmins has published fiction and poetry nationally. She performs her poetry with musicians, fire-eaters, and dancers, and has released a CD, *Iowa Summer*.

Barbara Crooker's *Ordinary Life* recently won the ByLine chapbook competition; other new books are *The White Poems* and *Paris*.

Loren Davidson is a writer, healer, ceremonialist, and permaculturist currently residing in northern California. He has walked an eclectic spiritual path for over thirty years.

Marjorie Carlson Davis's writing focuses in some way on the human–nature connection. Her poetry has most recently appeared in *Voices Along the River,* published by the Kellogg Environmental Center. Fiction is forthcoming in *Stories from Where We Live, Many Mountains Moving,* and *Frontiers: A Journal of Women Studies*.

Lucille Lang Day's poetry collections are *Infinities, Wild One, Fire in the Garden,* and *Self-Portrait with Hand Microscope*. She has also published a chapbook.

Joyce Derzaph is married, with a beautiful little daughter and a cat. She has been writing poetry since she was a child.

Corinne De Winter has been nominated twice for the Pushcart Prize and has appeared in more than six hundred publications, along with publishing seven collections of poetry and prose. She lives in western Massachusetts.

Danny DiCrispino has been published in *Poetry Motel, Abbey,* and *Beginnings*. He also won second prize in the Baltimore County Public Schools writing contest in 2002.

Deborah Dill currently lives and works in the city, but still dreams of a green hillside with sheep.

Karen Donnally was a member of circles both sacred and informal, and a therapist who also coordinated services for low-income women and their families. Before her death on August 29, 2002, she lived with her sixteen-year-old son in Pennsylvania.

Alexa Duir lives in Herefordshire, England.

John J. Dunphy has published his haiku in the journals and anthologies of every English-speaking nation, as well as in translation in Japan and China.

Tish Eastman's poetry has won prizes from *Poetry in Windows IV* and *San Gabriel Valley Poets Quarterly.* She was a featured reader at the LA Poetry Festival.

Louis Elvira has been on a Pagan path his entire life of more than forty years and finds that he has only just begun to appreciate life and death. Most recently, he has been HP of a quiet coven, the Dun, finding both joy and grief.

Karen Ethelsdattar is poet, liturgist, and ritual maker whose work affirms women and the feminine presence of God. Her first collection of poems was *Earthwalking & Other Poems,* 2001.

Maureen Tolman Flannery grew up a rancher's daughter in Wyoming, is infatuated with the rich complexity of Mexico, and has published two books of poetry, along with editing an anthology of travel poetry, *Knowing Stones: Poems of Exotic Places.*

CB Follett's fourth collection of poetry, *At the Turning of the Light,* won the 2001 National Poetry Book Award. Nominated for five Pushcart Prizes, she is publisher/co-editor of *Runes, A Review of Poetry.*

Bethanie Frank is a theater and communications professor at Coffeyville Community College in Kansas. "Prayer to Arachne" is part of a collection honoring women in Greek mythology.

Clay Gilbert is working on an M.F.A. in creative writing at the University of South Carolina, where he is also an instructor in the first-year English program. His current project is a novel, *Dark Road to Paradise.*

John Gilgun is the author of, most recently, *The Dooley Poems* (Robin Price, 1991) and *Your Buddy Misses You* (Three Phase, 1995).

Natalie Green is a writer and poet who follows the path of natural druidry. Her work is inspired by nature and the changing seasons.

Leigh Griffith, a practicing Pagan since 1969 and a Maine resident for twenty-one years, creates art quilts and poetry in Houlton, Maine.

Tony Grist was born in 1951 and with his wife, Aileen, runs a coven in Oldham, England. They are co-authors of *The Illustrated Guide to Wicca* (Godsfield Press).

Margaret Hammitt-McDonald (Moonheart) is a medical student, former English teacher, and future doula who lives in Oregon with a life partner, an organic garden, and eight kitties.

Tim Harkins retired from the U.S. Navy in 1995 and has worked as a technical writer since. He is a member of Ord Brighideach (3rd shift, Ash Cill) and a proud grandfather.

Carey Harrison is studying art history in Virginia and plans to pursue further education in theater and English literature.

Cher Holt-Fortin, mother, grandmother, crone, lives in central New York. In addition to writing, she quilts and practices a martial art. She recently won the Moonfire prize for women's poetry with her chapbook, *Waving a Banana Leaf.*

Ava M. Hu just completed her M.F.A. in poetry at the New School in New York City. She is currently working on a book-length work of poems based on the Siddhartha story, with the protagonist as a woman.

Deborah Hunter has had poems published in numerous publications, including *Nimrod, Curbside Review,* and

Another Sun, and in several anthologies. Originally from Tulsa, Oklahoma, she now resides in Houston, Texas.

Charlotte Hussey, an OBOD member who teaches creative writing at McGill University, has published *Rue Sainte Famille* (Vehicule, 1990) and *The Head Will Continue to Sing* (Over the Moon, 2000).

Carrie Jankeloff-Edelstein is a free-spirited earthworshipper, spending most of her days encouraging growth and magickal awareness in her beautiful daughter while still trying to find the strength to exist on a planet where apathy and spiritual numbness abound.

Jennifer Johnson, a writer and teacher, lives in Calforina with her husband and two spoiled cats. Her poems have appeared in various publications.

Birgitta Jonsdottir lives in Iceland and has taken part in art and poetry festivals around the world. She is editor for the global anthologies *The Book of Hope* and *The World Healing Book.*

Kay Jordan is an Arizona-based writer who has published short stories, poetry, and essays. She is working on a ghost story, and loves to write, read, knit, and travel.

Raven Kaldera is a farmer, homesteader, pagan minister, intersex FTM activist, and homeschooling parent. He is the author of *Hermaphrodeities: The Transgender Spirituality Workbook* and co-author of *The Urban Primitive.*

Bridget Kelley-Lossada recently earned her M.F.A. in poetry from Antioch University. Her poetry has appeared in *51%, Inkwell,* and in the e-journal *Moondance.*

Susan Kennedy's *Dancing with the Dog* was published by Philos Press in 2002. *Cazadera Poems* (with Mike Tuggle) was published by Floating Island Publications.

Robert Lord Keyes is town archivist for Pelham, Massachusetts. His work has appeared in *Massachusetts Review, Passages North, Beloit Poetry Journal,* and other publications.

Will Killhour is a retired master mariner who lives and teaches in Montpelier, Vermont.

Rudyard Kipling (1865–1936) was born in Bombay and became famous for his poems and stories celebrating the heroism of British soldiers in India and Burma. He was the first Englishman to win the Nobel Prize for Literature (1907).

Galina Krasskova is currently gythia of Urdabrunnr Kindred and a devoted Odin's woman. She has been ordained within the Fellowship of Isis and is a graduate of the New Seminary, where she was ordained as an interfaith minister.

K. A. Laity is a medievalist at the University of Houston Downtown. Her novel *Pelzmantel* (Spilled Candy, 2003) weaves medieval history with fairy tales and witchcraft.

Kathleen Landerman is a practicing oneiromancer and lives on a farm with eighteen cats and a herd of reindeer. Or not.

Susan Landon's poetry has appeared in many publications, including the anthologies *Rising to the Dawn, We Speak for Peace,* and *Freedom's Just Another Word.*

Judith Laura is author of *Goddess Spirituality for the 21st Century* (1997), *She Lives! The Return of Our Great Mother* (1989), and *Three Part Invention,* a novel (2002).

Dorothy Laurence lives by a tidal river in Ipswich, Massachusetts, where she writes poetry. She is founder of the Ipswich Poetry Group.

Erynn Rowan Laurie is a writer and professional crazy woman living in Seattle, where she practices *filidecht,* an early Irish form of sacred poetry.

Ellen Lindquist of Atlanta is a Pushcart Prize–nominated poet whose work has appeared in *Pif* Magazine, *the cafe irreal, 5 AM,* and others.

Gizmo LittleWing has been writing all her life, loves new experiences, and is continuing her education. This is her first publication.

John Litzenberg (Greybeard Dances) is a musician, poet, writer, philosopher and lifelong pagan currently living in New Orleans with his soul mate Starlight Dances, artist, herbalist, and magickal gardener.

Laura Loomis is a social worker in the San Francisco area, looking for a publisher for her novel about child protective work.

Naomi Ruth Lowinsky's poetry has been widely published most recently in *Rattle, Many Mountains Moving, Colere, Paterson Literary Review,* and *Dark Moon Lilith.* Her book *red clay is talking* was published by Scarlet Tanager in 2000. She is a Jungian analyst.

Melisande Luna is a student of geology in central California, who enjoys blending science with poetry. Her work has been published in *Poetry Sz, The Bakersfield Californian, Mi Pos ezine, Fluid Ink Press, Divine Pleasures,* and *The Freelancer.*

Judy Clark McCann lives in rural Pennsylvania. Her poems have appeared in several anthologies and journals, plus a book of collected works. She finds her true voice through the study of myth and depth psychology.

Margaret McCarthy's poetry has appeared in a variety of publications. Her play *The Sacrificial King: A Play for John Lennon* was produced in New York, where she lives and works as a photographer. Her landscape studies and photographs based on Celtic mythology have been exhibited widely.

C. Leigh McGinley is a Keltrian Druid of the Ring of the Oak. She is a former elementary school teacher and currently works as an environmental consultant for a large waste-management company.

Eileen Malone lives and writes every day in the coastal fog of the necropolis of Colma, where San Francisco buries its dead.

Jeff Mann has published fiction, essays, and poetry in many literary magazines and anthologies. He teaches creative writing and Appalachian studies at Virginia Tech.

M. P. Mann, lover of myths and legends, and student of shamanism, lives in rural Ohio with her family.

mbtucker, formerly "Wynter MacLeod" in magical circles, writes from her home in the farmlands of south central Pennsylvania. She has taught and participated in local Pagan community and the larger MidAtlantic Reclaiming community for ten years.

Frank Miller is a retired English teacher who lives on the Washington coast. His work has appeared in such journals as *Wavelength, Rain,* and *580-Split*.

MaryJane Millington is a twenty-three-year-old college graduate who has been researching and occasionally practicing Wicca since she was fifteen. She has been published previously in *The Dickinson Review*.

Anna Mills is a Pagan Quaker Jew who writes poetry, essays, and memoir. She has been hiking in Yosemite every summer since she was ten.

Tara Moghadam's poetry has been published in *Kalliope, The Southern Poetry Review, Phantasmagoria,* and other journals. She lives in Minnesota with her three children, two cats, and the two dogs that follow her religiously from room to room.

MoonSongstress is an English hedgewitch. She is married with no children but has a cat with enormous teeth and six very well guarded goldfish.

Patricia Monaghan's *Seasons of the Witch* won the Friends of Literature Award for poetry in 1994. Her nonfiction books include *The Book of Goddesses and Heroines*.

Rita Moran, having left a former life in public safety, photojournalism, music, and teaching in ghetto schools, is enjoying life as a bookseller and Pagan/community activist.

The Mystic Fool is a 34-year-old male, Solitary Eclectic Wiccan from Westchester, New York. He practices/studies folk magick, divination, and Wiccan ritual magick.

Andrew Nicoll is a married father of three, a reporter, living in a big old Victorian house by the beach at Dundee, Scotland.

Yolanda Nieves is a teacher, writer, and mystic who lives in Chicago.

Jessica Jordan Nudel is a writer and educator from Charlottesville, Virginia. She has published two collections: *The Season of Leaving* (awarded a Sarasota Poetry Press award) and *In Jenna's Dream* (awarded a Heekin Foundation fellowship).

Annette Opalczynski's poetry has appeared in *The Sun* and *The Paterson Literary Review*. She has received a grant from the Delaware Division of the Arts.

Burrowing (P.B.) Owl is a Shamanic and Wiccan initiate with fifteen thousand books, mean cats, and an understanding wife. His work appears regularly in *PagaNet News*.

Memory Peterson-Baur is an Iowan, and so was the little black cat she writes about. She spends her time gardening, hiking, getting involved in public affairs, and writing poetry.

Tina Petrakis is a medical writer for the biopharmaceutical industry. Her poetry won the Judges' Special Prize in the 2001 Dorothy Dutcher Literary Competition.

Karen Porter lives in a house of many critters in the haunted Pinelands of southern New Jersey, home of white sand, black water, and the infamous Jersey Devil.

Lauren Raine has been a sacred maskmaker, performance artist, writer, and ritualist for twenty-five years. In 1999 she created *The Masks of the Goddess* for the Spiral Dance in San Francisco; in 2001, she directed *The Masque of the Goddess,* a continually evolving community ritual play.

E. W. Richardson is a Marine Vietnam veteran and editor of *Distant Echoes,* a literary journal. He lives in California.

Eric Robbins, an independent bookseller in his native land of central Maine, enjoys many creative pursuits and works for positive change in his Pagan and secular communities.

Julie Robertson (dryadsage) has practiced eclectic Wicca for approximately ten years. She has a B.S. in psychology, religious studies, and sociology, and currently lives in southern California.

Marina Rubin grew up in Vinnitsa, Ukraine, and came to the United States in 1989. Her poetry has appeared in various literary magazines and journals such as *Visions International, 5 AM,* and *Poetry Motel.*

Helen Ruggieri lives in Olean, New York. Her chapbook, *The Character for Woman,* was published by Foot Hills Publishing; her poetry chapbook, *Glimmer Girls,* is available from Mayapple Press.

Dennis Saleh's poetry, prose, and artwork appear widely in magazines and anthologies. In 2002, he read from his work at the Rosicrucian Egyptian Museum in San Jose, California.

Lawrence Schimel is a full-time author and anthologist who has published more than forty books, including *Tarot Fantastic, The Fortune Tellers, The Drag Queen of Elfland, Things Invisible to See: Lesbian and Gay Tales of Magic Realism,* and *Blood Lines: Vampire Stories from New England.*

Jennifer Schneider lives and writes in Missoula, Montana.

Ann K. Schwader lives and writes in Westminster, Colorado. Her collection of dark SF poetry, *Architectures of Night,* was recently published by Dark Regions Press.

Art Schwartz's poems and memoirs have appeared in numerous publications, including *The Classical Outlook* and *The Connecticut River Review,* and five of his plays have been produced in New York, where he lives.

Seabhacgheal is a member of Ár nDraíocht Féin, the Order of the White Oak, and Phoenix Coven in Norwich, Connecticut.

Selchie, a weaver of words equally at home diving into silence, practices the magic of earth healing through poetry, gardening, street actions, and play therapy.

Arthur Slate lives and writes in Vermont.

Laurence Snydal is a poet, musician, and retired teacher whose poetry has appeared in several magazines and anthologies. He is the author of two books for new fathers.

Maryanne Stahl casts her spells beside a small lake outside Atlanta, where she teaches writing at Kennesaw State University. Her first novel, *Forgive the Moon,* was published in 2002 and her second, *The Opposite Shore,* in 2003.

Cassie Premo Steele divides her time between the American South and the Irish West, and writes on the healing of women's bodies and spirits.

Jean Sinclair Symmes is a clinical psychologist by profession and a poet by obsession. She is also a playwright who occasionally gets produced.

Doreen Valiente may be rightly termed one of the founders of modern Wicca. Initiated by Gerald Gardner in 1953, she became known as a talented writer who gave freely of her talent to help foster the growing religion. She died in 1999.

Marianne Wade is poet, pagan, teacher, and tarot teacher. She hosts poetry workshops on America Online, and her poems have appeared in *Samsara, Baker Street Irregular, The Writer's Hood,* and on *Poetry Talk.* She lives in south San Francisco.

Candace Walworth lives in Boulder, Colorado, where she teaches at Naropa University.

Sarah Brown Weitzman has been published in many journals, including a "Featured Poet" appearance in *Tendrils.* She is the recipient of an NEA fellowship and has twice been a finalist in the Academy of American Poets' Walt Whitman Award contest.

Patricia Wellingham-Jones is a two-time Pushcart Prize nominee, author of *Don't Turn Away: Poems About Breast Cancer* and *Apple Blossoms at Eye Level.*

Cynthia West is an internationally collected painter as well as a poet who lives in Santa Fe.

Anthony Russell White lives in San Rafael, California, serves on the permanent staff of the Nine Gates Mystery School and has been writing poetry (again) since 1992.

Sophie M. White is a poet and editorial cartoonist for *The New Albany* (Indiana) *Tribune* and a "professional aunt and great-aunt."

Daniel Williams, a poet of the Sierra Nevada mountain region of California, has read recently at the Frye Museum of Art in Seattle.

Beau Williamson is a writer of stories and Celtic-influenced artist in Montreal who has practiced "extreme eclectic" paganism for the past fifteen years.

Bonnie Wodin lives in Heath, Massachusetts (among the Heath-ens), and is a landscape designer, workshop leader, and writer.

William Wordsworth (1770–1850) was one of England's foremost writers of the Romantic period and often celebrated nature in his work.

William Butler Yeats (1865–1939), winner of the 1923 Nobel Prize for Literature, was a prolific poet active in late-nineteenth-century magical groups and in the cause of Irish independence.

Rena Yount has published poetry, nonfiction, and occasional fiction, and currently lives in Washington, D.C.

CREDITS

The life of a poet is often lonely and very seldom lucrative. Many poets must be content with seeing their work in print, and receive little or no remuneration for their words. Out of respect for the poets who have offered their work for publication here, I ask my readers to use good sense in their use of these works.

If you wish to incorporate one of the poems in this book into a ritual for yourself or a private gathering, you are absolutely free to do so, and most poets would be honored to have their work so used. When you write down the ritual for private use, it is a good idea to note the name of the original author. If you change the poem to better suit your purpose, note that it is "adapted from" the original work by the original author.

If you wish to use one of these poems at a large open gathering, particularly an event that people have paid to attend, it is legally and ethically right to contact the poet first and ask permission. Be sure to credit the writer and refrain from adapting the poem without permission.

If you wish to republish the poem in any public written form—for instance, if you want to include it on your Web site or in your local Pagan newsletter—copyright law requires that you get written permission from the author, who is free to require a special copyright notice, charge a fee, or simply say no.

Whether it is legal or not, it is always unethical to use someone else's words without credit. Please honor the craft of these poets by using their work respectfully.

The following is a list of permissions and first-publication notices for some of the poems in this book. Even if you don't see a poem listed in this section, the author still holds the copyright and all the restrictions mentioned here apply.

"The Candle" by JoAnn Anglin: First published in *Koleinu,* the newsletter of Temple B'nai Israel in Sacramento.

"Treehood" by Archer: First published in *Avalon Rising,* Lammas 1999.

"The Charge of the God" by Archer: First published in *Reclaiming Quarterly,* summer 2002.

"Romancing the Crone" by Dorothy Bates: Previously published in *Crone Chronicles* and *Creations.*

"Beltane" by Geraldine Moorkens Byrne: First published in the monthly pagan poetry ezine *Pagan Poetry Pages.*

"My Lover Gives the Five-Fold Kiss" and "A Bawdy Song" by Kiwi Carlisle: First published in the author's self-distributed chapbook.

"Elemental Blessings" by Kiwi Carlisle: Previously published (without permission) on PODSnet and later the Internet as part of a ritual by Mike Fix.

"For a Friend Lying in Intensive Care, Waiting for her White Blood Cells to Rejuvenate after a Bone Marrow Transplant" by Barbara Crooker: First appeared in *Poets On* (1994); also published in the author's *The White Poems.*

"Predators" by Loren Davidson: First published on the author's Web site.

"Snake Dance" by Lucille Lang Day: Previously published in the author's collection, *Fire in the Garden.*

"To In Daghda, Summer, 2001" by Alexa Duir: First published October 2001 in *Pagan Dawn* magazine.

"six months pregnant" by John J. Dunphy: First published in *Brussels Sprout* VII:2.

"Honor to the Goddess, Lady of Many Names" by Karen Ethelsdattar: First published in Starhawk's book *The Spiral Dance,* HarperSanFrancisco, and later in Ethelsdattar's second collection of poems, *Thou Art a Woman & Other Poems,* 2002.

"Worshiping Gods" by Fred and Leigh: First published in *Enchanté,* 1997.

"How to Be a Shaman 2" by John Gilgun: First published in *Kimera: A Journal of Fine Writing,* Volume 5 (Spokane, Wash., 2000).

"Tree Song" by Natalie Green: Previously published in *Touchstone.*

"The Green Man is Watching Us" by Leigh Griffith: First published in *The Blessed Bee,* Fall 2002.

"Black Kali" by Deborah Hunter: First published in the author's chapbook, *The Moon and Other Deities.*

"Imbolc Eve" by Jennifer Johnson: First published in *Pan-Gaia,* Winter 01–02.

"The Garden of Idunn" by Birgitta Jonsdottir: First published in the author's book *Wake Up,* 2001.

"The Womb" by Kay Jordan: First published in the journal *Island* (Australia) in 1990.

"Hymn to Athena" by Raven Kaldera: First published in *Hermaphrodeities: The Transgender Spirituality Workbook.*

"Erce: Earth Goddess," edited and translated by K. A. Laity: Previously published in *Avalon Rising* 1.3, 1999, and *Seeker Journal* 13.2, 2001.

"Waning Moon Invocation" by Judith Laura: Reprinted from *Goddess Spirituality for the 21st Century: From Kabbalah to Quantum Physics* © 1997 by Judith Laura. All rights reserved. Used with permission of the author.

"Shapechanger" by Eileen Malone: First published in *The Typewriter* (San Francisco).

"The Sacrifice" by C. Leigh McGinley: Previously published in *Henge Happenings*.

"Shiva to Kali, on the Charnel Ground" and "Kali to Shiva, on the Charnel Ground" by Patricia Monaghan: First published in *Dancing with Chaos* by Patricia Monaghan (Salmon Poetry, 2002).

"Branch and Bone" by Rita Moran: First published in *EarthTides Pagan Network News*.

"the dandelion woman" by Jessica Jordan Nudel: Prize winner in the NFSPS Women's Poetry Award.

"Handfasting" by Julie Robertson: First published on the poet's personal Web site.

"Oath of Scribes" by Dennis Saleh: Previously published in *Wavelength*.

"Oblation" by Dennis Saleh: Published in *Psychological Perspectives*.

"Papyrus Wine" by Dennis Saleh: Published in *Great River Review*.

"The Hound of Ulster" by Lawrence Schimel: First published in *Isaac Asimov's Science Fiction Magazine*, March 1995.

"To Socrates, on the State of Philosophy in the Suburbs" by Art Schwartz: First published in the *Connecticut River Review*.

"Taking the Earth as a Lover" by Selchie: First published in *A Poem Can Do That,* 2002.

"Red Candle" and "Diamonds" by Maryanne Stahl: Originally published in *Poetry* magazine, April 2002.

"first fruits" by mbtucker: First published in *SageWoman,* Autumn 1995.

"Charge of the Goddess" by Doreen Valiente: Copyright John Belham-Payne, The Centre for Pagan Studies.

"Vigil" by Sarah Brown Weitzman: First published in *New American Review,* Spring 1982.

"Heartstone" by Patricia Wellingham-Jones: Published in *Manzanita Quarterly,* Autumn 2001, and in *Labyrinth: Poems Prose,* edited by Patricia Wellingham-Jones, 2001.

"Counting My Feathers" by Anthony Russell White: First published in *Clackamas Literary Review,* IV:2, Fall/Winter 2000.

INDEX OF AUTHORS, TITLES, AND FIRST LINES

꙳ ꙳ ꙳

ABOUT THE EDITOR

Jane Raeburn is the author of *Celtic Wicca* and co-author (with Cynthia Jane Collins) of *Building a Magical Relationship*. A writer, editor and Web-site producer, Jane crafts public and private rituals as priestess of the Temple of Brigantia in southern Maine. For seven years she wrote "Jane's Tidings," a compilation of Wiccan and Pagan news items. She wrote her first poem at age four, and spent part of her later career writing newspaper headlines, which are their own form of poetry. To learn more, visit her Web site at www.janeraeburn.com.